THE SECRET LIFE OF
CORPORATIONS

*Understanding the True Nature
of Business*

Mark I. Sirkin, PhD

THE SECRET LIFE OF CORPORATIONS
UNDERSTANDING THE TRUE NATURE OF BUSINESS

iUniverse books may be ordered through booksellers or by contacting:

iUniverse
1663 Liberty Drive
Bloomington, IN 47403
www.iuniverse.com
1-800-Authors (1-800-288-4677)

Because of the dynamic nature of the Internet, any web addresses or links contained in this book may have changed since publication and may no longer be valid. The views expressed in this work are solely those of the author and do not necessarily reflect the views of the publisher, and the publisher hereby disclaims any responsibility for them.

Any people depicted in stock imagery provided by Thinkstock are models, and such images are being used for illustrative purposes only. Certain stock imagery © Thinkstock.

ISBN: 978-1-4917-2924-3 (sc)
ISBN: 978-1-5320-8467-6 (hc)
ISBN: 978-1-4917-2925-0 (e)

Print information available on the last page.

iUniverse rev. date: 03/10/2020

CONTENTS

PREFACE TO THE SECOND EDITION

Starting with the basics, this book takes a biological and evolutionary view of corporations, rather than approaching them solely from an economic or financial point of view. The most fundamental ideas are these:

- Organizations are living systems
- All living systems have common characteristics
  o Living systems have structures (i.e., form)
  o Living systems engage in processes (i.e., function)
- Living systems tend to cluster in communities of similar individuals
- Living systems exist in ecosystems in which they compete for resources

Not particularly complicated or sophisticated ... yet. Just another way of seeing something that all of us happen to be intimately familiar with—the modern corporation. We buy from them every day, we invest in them, they are in the news, most of us work for them in one way or another, and some of us consult with them, trying to help them and their members accomplish the tasks they set before themselves. As we dig deeper to try to understand corporations as living organisms, we encounter the axioms of dynamic systems theory (an amalgam of the several extant versions of systems theory) that help us make sense of this economic organism.

Dynamic systems theory (DST) utilizes *axioms of structure* that enable us to understand corporate organisms. First, in what is sometimes called the Matrioschka principle, the levels of systems go from simple to complex, each level consisting of similar types at the same level. For example, consider cells, tissues, organs, and bodies as a metaphor, or people, teams, departments, and companies in a corporation, as Russian dolls stacked one inside the other. Each system (a system can be any organization of parts) has boundaries that contain it (remember the semi-permeable membrane of a cell from high school biology?). Subsystems within larger systems differentiate over time and become specialized. These differentiated parts often develop hierarchical relationships in which some parts control others. These are the so-called axioms of structure in DST.

How these organisms interact with the outside world comprise the *axioms of process* in DST. Development is an axiom that suggests maturation of an organism over time. Growth is what happens to organisms (taken individually) or populations (taken in the context of the ecosystem). Finally, change happens for a variety of reasons, often in response to external conditions, but these changes are just as often nonlinear and sudden. They are not, for the most part, predictable in a specific sense.

Taken together, these are the core aspects of DST. The first five chapters of this book discuss these concepts and many others in great detail.

Why a second edition, and why now? It's been over 15 years since this book was first published. Self-published and virtually ignored, I have come to the sad conclusion that either I've done an inadequate job explaining these ideas or the world is not yet ready for or interested in them. So my first impulse was to hire an editor to help rewrite the text in a more comprehensible version. I know these are not simple concepts and require at least a passing knowledge of several arcane subjects: systems theory, evolutionary biology, and psychoanalysis to name just a few. As the editor and I worked together, we both concluded that complex ideas sometimes require complex language to explain them. While we could tweak some sentences here and there, there is no getting around the fact that this book would never be a simple or quick read.

Even more of a barrier than simplification was the fact that the book was written in the early 2000s, before the tremendous popularity of Facebook and Google, the beginning of Twitter, and the founding of some of the biggest companies extant. At the time of writing, FAANG stocks—Facebook, Amazon, Apple, Netflix, Google—dominate the marketplace, with some of their cousins in China and elsewhere not far behind (e.g., Baidu, Huawei, Tencent, and so on). The examples in the first edition, while still relevant to those who know this history, needed to be thoroughly replaced to be relevant to a new generation, or even to the marketplace today.

Faced with these two barriers, and not wanting to wait another 15 years, I have decided to republish the book with very few changes. The words of one of the most prolific business writers, Peter Drucker, kept ringing in my ears. He said something along the lines of "I never reread my books; why do that when I can use that time to write another one?"

Don't get me wrong. I think the science is still sound, the ideas are sound, and the viewpoint of organizations as living systems is as true today as when I first wrote about these ideas all those years ago. Indeed, I have continued to lecture, present these concepts, and develop them. However, most people with whom I speak are still not ready to take the step of viewing corporations as living systems—not metaphorically, but actually. I continue to believe corporations, all companies really, are living systems, literally alive, and I utilize these ideas in my consulting work on a daily basis. As the approach has developed, I have also acknowledged that governments, religions, and colleges are also complex, corporate, living systems but of a different sort (species? phylum? kingdom?) than business corporations. Not-for-profit companies can look like, and be structured as, any of the above four types.

I have decided to add a new, final chapter in recognition of some interesting developments that are emerging in the public understanding of corporations. This is Chapter 14. For those of you who tried the earlier version, I hope the new chapter re-presents these ideas in a fresh light. For those new to these concepts, enjoy the ride. It is indeed a Brave New World where people will vie with corporations for control of their destinies. If we know anything for sure, it is that life will continue to proliferate in all its wonderful. unpredictable variety. Now corporations and other multibody systems can fully join the parade.

Mark I. Sirkin
White Plains, NY
December 2019

PREFACE

As a working psychologist and business consultant, I have tried to make this book a unique marriage of innovative business theory and practical business recommendations.

My interpretation of the contemporary company as a living organism is no mere metaphor, nor is it the language of the latest management fad. I believe that business is, quite literally, biological at its core.

Psychologist's Journey, Consultant's Perspective: Some Biographical Considerations

I have been an applied systems psychologist since I began practicing psychology in the late 1970s. There was not then, nor is there now, a distinct subdiscipline called "systems psychology." I leave it to the reader to follow the connecting threads that have led me to dynamic systems theory and the biodynamic approach.

My intellectual journey to understand human systems began with my fascination with biology and philosophy. These were subjects that I pursued for fun while in high school. Also during this time, I was in an accelerated program that taught the principles of biology from an ecological perspective, as opposed to the more traditional biochemical or taxonomic approaches.

I left high school early to begin college at Boston University, where I met a remarkable philosopher named Peter Bertocci. He was a unique individual who, as the Borden Parker Bowne Professor of Philosophy, combined the fields of psychology and theology, ethics and metaphysics. He taught the only undergraduate course in the philosophy of personality in the country, and I was lucky to have studied with him for four years.

While at Boston University, I encountered another remarkable thinker, Sigmund Koch, who as a young scholar had edited a multivolume study of psychology at mid-century that still stands as one of the towering intellectual achievements in the field. Koch was a brilliant iconoclast who, throughout his career, was among psychology's harshest critics.

Finally at BU, Michael Fleming, who introduced me to the complexities of psychoanalytic theory, mentored me. With Michael, I published my first paper on psychoanalytic theory, looking specifically at Freud's earliest attempts to create a scientific psychology.

These three thinkers represent my intellectual touchstones and early influences, from which the biodynamic approach has grown.

I attended graduate school at the University of Connecticut, where the cognitive-behavioral hostility toward psychoanalysis gave me the opportunity to be an iconoclast myself within our school microcosm of psychology. Family therapy and, separately, my interest in theories of emotion and hypnosis were areas of study where I could learn the craft of psychotherapy and study applied personality without feeling that I had to compromise the psychodynamic ideas that had become most important to my understanding of people. Here, I was introduced to systems theory during a course in family therapy. Systems theory became a neutral ground where the often-conflicting ideas of cognitive psychology, psychoanalysis, family therapy, and emotion theory could cross-fertilize one another.

After graduate school, I spent my clinical internship at the Jewish Board of Family and Children's Services in New York City. I went to New York because it was the bastion of psychoanalysis, and the Jewish Board was among the best of the best, especially for someone like me, interested in working with children.

I learned an important lesson that year about human systems: Individual behavior is meaningless out of context.[1] As I tried to work with individual children and their psychological problems, I discovered something that changed my thinking and practice permanently. No matter what I did with a child for one hour per week, she or he went back to a family for the other hundred and sixty-seven hours. The implication, clearly, was that for the child to change, the family had to change. Facilitating such change was not a simple challenge. It required years of study in the art and science of systems change at the family level.

I was fortunate to have studied with some of the great names in the family therapy field: Clifford Sager and Salvador Minuchin while in New York; then with Lyman Wynne, Duke Stanton, Judy Landau, and Susan McDaniel when I joined the faculty at the University of Rochester Medical Center. I learned that craft well. By the time I stopped working with families therapeutically, I

---

[1] Psychoanalysis is based on a deep understanding of the individual. The structural theory is, in fact, a type of systems theory, if we view the id, ego, and superego as the components of each individual's psychological system. I believed then, and still do, that there is no more sophisticated theory for understanding the psychology of individuals as individuals. But in an applied setting, where individuals interact and form social systems, it is woefully incomplete. See Chapter 5 for a fuller discussion of these issues.

had seen hundreds of them with a wide variety of problems and challenges. I developed special skills and insights working with families who were caught in destructive cult groups and with families who struggled with the disruption that intermarriage sometimes brings (Sirkin, 1990a; Sirkin & Wynne, 1990; Sirkin 1994a, 1994b).

As much as I enjoyed working with families, I became increasingly fascinated by the complexity of other human systems. While on the faculty at the University of Rochester, I learned about and worked with groups of patients. I was appointed director of group research and training in the department of psychiatry, studying groups as well as family systems. I began to see cults as pathological groups and uncovered some of the processes at the heart of group dysfunction (Sirkin, 1990b). It became clear to me that if cults were among the worst examples of group pathology, then the best, most productive groups could be found in corporate systems.

After marrying (my own ongoing experiment in family and group psychology), I found myself back in New York City and enrolled in a new program, under the auspices of Laurence Gould, at the William Alanson White Psychoanalytic Institute. The institute taught organizational consulting and development from a psychodynamic perspective. This was the perfect segue for me, because I had been teaching many of these same theories in Rochester as they applied to therapeutic groups. Now I was learning how to apply them in an organizational environment. I found the world of organizations fascinating and challenging.

As I transitioned my practice from family psychotherapy to organizational consulting, I developed an expertise in working with family businesses, the perfect combination of organizational and family system challenges (Sirkin, 1996). Although well suited to my background, I found family businesses ultimately too confining. I was looking for a larger stage.

I left clinical practice and joined a consulting firm in 1994, and have not looked back since. In that time I have worked with scores of companies in dozens of industries. In many respects, this book represents what I have learned during that journey.

Dynamic systems theory (DST) is my attempt to explore the ramifications of this idiosyncratic amalgam of ideas. It is a robust systems theory that is useful to understand psychological behavior in groups and organizations.

DST gives us a new understanding of a wide range of phenomena, from organizational behavior to organizational design. It invites us to consider business in the context of other human endeavors, and to understand how, courtesy of global business, we have entered an entirely new phase in the evolutionary history of life on this planet.

The idea of corporation as organism stands in stark contrast to that of corporation as machine, one of our culture's most deeply embedded and enduring constructs. It is also a construct that, in my thinking, is now outdated. From lean, mean organizational structures to reengineered corporate processes, from organizational designs to corporate control mechanisms, the corporation has in recent years been portrayed as a complex system that can become a fine-tuned profit machine. I propose that a *biological* perspective offers many advantages over this mechanistic view.

Part I of this book, "*The Theoretical Framework*," is an explanation of my biodynamic interpretation of business, and of human organizations in general. By "biodynamic," I mean to suggest that an organization is a living system with all the characteristics of life that any organism might exhibit. There are social, economic, and personal implications to these ideas, all touched on in the pages that follow.

This section introduces my concept of a "fourth kingdom" of life on earth. That is, while the first three biological kingdoms are represented respectively by plants, animals, and the unseen microscopic world, I put forward that human social systems constitute a next, wholly separate, evolutionary level—a *fourth kingdom*.

Part II, *"The Challenges to Come: A Consultant's Perspective,"* is a collection of observational essays in the reflective style of one of my intellectual heroes, the late Stephen Jay Gould. In these essays, I take on a variety of contemporary business topics— corporate governance, CEO effectiveness, family businesses, myths of leadership, and the consulting and psychology professions themselves—and view them through the lens of biodynamic theory. This approach provides a platform to discuss a number of interrelated themes and concepts. Taken together, these themes build upon each other and provide a powerful set of ideas for consultants, business executives, economists, and social scientists.

My hope is that biodynamic theory will elucidate a number of business challenges, the better to cope with and successfully surmount them. I trust the theorist and the lay business reader alike will find this biological perspective enlightening and useful.

Important Terms

For the reader's convenience, I will briefly identify here some of the key terms I've used in this book.

Biodynamics: A philosophy, perspective, or worldview that includes all of the following terms as key ideas, and entails the belief and commitment that organizations are best understood as living entities.

Dynamic Systems Theory: A set of theoretical propositions that explains the workings of all complex living systems, from organisms to organizations.

Fourth Kingdom: A biological, taxonomic classification that enables us to view organizations as living systems, comparable to animals, plants, and protozoa.

Functional Anatomy: An approach to organizational design that permits a functional analysis of a company's key areas: e.g., finance, manufacturing, human resources.

Meaning Communities: Social organizations comprised of psychological and emotional layers that give them stability and predictability.

Organizational Ecosystem: A system of systems that constitute the economy and help us understand the context in which organizations grow, succeed, or fail.

ACKNOWLEDGMENTS

In a writing project such as this one, which has taken so long to complete, it is hard to know where to begin and whom to thank first. The first thank-you undoubtedly goes to friends and colleagues who not only encouraged me, but discussed many of the ideas found here in their earliest form. Special thanks to Barry Berg, Mary Kralj, Cynthia Leeds Friedlander, Joel Mausner, Victoria Brush, and Mitchell Scherr, for whose encouragement I will always be grateful.

I can truly say that this book would still be struggling to find the light of day without the invaluable editorial assistance of Mark Gauthier. More than an editor, more than a midwife, Mark and his enthusiastic, unflagging support made this book a reality. A special thanks to Larry Leichman, who knew just when to push and when to cajole to help move the project along.

A great big hug of thanks to my family, especially Roshana, Gabriel, and Maia, my three children, who would arrive early in the morning or late at night only to find Dad hard at work on The Book. Perseverance pays, kids, and this is the proof. Knowing that this was as much a commitment to you as to myself helped get me through the more frustrating moments. And for my wife, Meri, who has been my rock-solid support in every way throughout this long endeavor. You are truly *my* woman of valor, whose price is well beyond rubies. This project has been with us almost as long as we have been together, and your encouragement and faith in me is something for which I will always be grateful. I guess we had that fourth child after all. I love you.

Finally, for my teachers and my clients, there is a little bit of all of you in here. I would not be who I am without you. My appreciation of your willingness to let me learn from you is boundless.

Mark I. Sirkin
White Plains, NY
September 2003

Part I

THE THEORETICAL FRAMEWORK

1
THE FOURTH KINGDOM

In this chapter, I explain the idea of the organization as organism, and place the approach firmly in a biological context. I spell out the biodynamic approach as a unique perspective on human social behavior. This chapter introduces the reader to systems theory in general and some specific versions in particular, and lays the groundwork for more detailed discussions.

The Grand Context

The history of life on the planet is a steady progression of growing complexity, punctuated by false starts, mass extinctions, and odd experiments. There have been dismal failures and spectacular successes; in some cases, the jury is still out.

As stated in the Preface, this book is about, in my opinion, the boldest experiment yet: a brand-new species evolving within a new taxonomic kingdom that represents the latest act in the grand pageant of life on the planet. This evolutionary experiment is changing the world as we know it and may ultimately sustain humanity's development beyond the confines of the biosphere. In this book, readers will find some new ideas alongside ideas that may seem obvious. There will be new ways of looking at common, observable facts. The discussion of business as biology may seem strange to many.

The Divisions of Life

Biologists use a variety of classification schemes to categorize life on earth. Early on, before the advent of the microscope, there were two taxonomic kingdoms: plants and animals. With the invention of the microscope, a whole new world opened, and a third kingdom was added: Protista.[1]

---

[1] Further scientific discoveries led to more sophisticated and elaborate schemes. Cells with a nucleus were determined to be significantly different from those without, and the entire living world was divided into two superkingdoms, eukaryotes and prokaryotes respectively. The discovery of viruses led to additional classification challenges.

Certainly the simplest and broadest division is between nucleated and nonnucleated organisms (Eukaryota and Prokaryota, respectively), although these two divisions are commonly known as superkingdoms. The next simplest grouping is a three-kingdom classification: multicellular animals (Animalia) and plants (Plantae), and single-cell monera (Monera), the latter representing bacteria and other nonnucleated organisms. Often viruses are considered to be a fourth kingdom in this schema, but including them raises some serious questions. Viruses are interesting but arguably retrograde, or derivative, life forms: "Viruses are completely devoid of the machinery for life processes; therefore, they could not have survived in the absence of cells" (Wagner, 1994–2000). Viruses are not viable organisms in their own right because they cannot survive without a host; therefore they don't meet the criteria of the second axiom of dynamic systems (see Chapter 2). To further complicate the picture, I suspect that computer viruses would actually qualify as real viruses, but since they don't infect life forms, are they alive? To close this discussion of viruses, let's agree to drop them from our classification of broad kingdoms.

Additional classification schemes include five kingdoms and even seven kingdoms for hard-to-classify groups such as blue-green algae, fungi, protozoans, and slime molds. Ultimately the work of classification is a science in itself. Whatever number we agree to work with—for our purposes, let's say three—this book is about the most recent branch on the phylogenetic tree of life.

Building upon this most basic classification scheme, I am proposing a fourth kingdom to include a particular form of human organization.

Throughout history, human beings have come together to form communities, tribes, or family groups, similar to those of our primate ancestors and the apes. *Recorded* history begins with the story of a particular kind of human group: the city-state. Although it is easy to see continuity from tribe to state, they are structurally quite different. The difference is analogous to that between a group of bugs and an ant colony. The colony functions as a coordinated, interdependent whole; so does the state. And so does the corporation.

The fourth kingdom includes corporate businesses as well as nation-states. Religions and universities are two additional forms of human organization. These are the four *phyla* of the fourth kingdom. *Phyla* are the basic divisions within a biological kingdom. The fourth kingdom is made up of *meaning communities*. People have a membership in such communities that is more psychological than physical. In most cases, people can elect to leave these communities, to join others, and often to join more than one.

This practice of cross-membership is especially acceptable among the four phyla. Within phyla, multiple memberships are less common and often discouraged. For example, one can be French, Catholic, a professor at the Sorbonne, and work for Société Générale; it is more difficult to be French and English, or work for Société Générale and Citibank.

These interactions will be touched upon, but the focus of this book is on one phylum of the fourth kingdom: *corporate businesses*.

To see the organization as an organism allows us to view corporate functions in terms of organic wholeness and integration, as a biologist understands anatomy and physiology. It enables us to approach organizational design based on the biological principles that underlie all living systems. In terms of the interactions among companies, this viewpoint enables us to view markets as dynamic ecosystems and industries as species that vie for capital resources in these financial ecosystems, or markets.

Defining the Biodynamic Approach

I use the term *biodynamics* to capture the unique biological perspective explored in the following pages.[2] The term covers a wide range of business and social phenomena.

Biodynamics is the point of view that living things can be usefully ordered on a scale from least to most complex. The species of organism that rests atop this pyramid of complexity is the corporate organization.

---

[2] *Biodynamics* is not a brand-new word, but I am using it in a new context with a new meaning. The *Oxford English Dictionary* defines biodynamics as "that part of biological science which treats of vital force, or the action of living organisms." These meanings are consistent with the roots of DST.

Recently, the term *biodynamics* has been used in two or three distinct ways. First, it refers to the study of the mechanics of fluid movement in the body, such as circulation, and is related to biomechanics. Second, the term has been used to describe a type of organic gardening and holistic farming (Thun, 2000). Most recently, a biodynamic approach to psychosomatic conditions has been outlined by Nunneley (2001). I will continue to use the term *biodynamic* to characterize a worldview rooted in DST for several reasons: it is an accurate use of the term as reflected in the OED definition, my first usage of it predates both Thun and Nunneley, and, most importantly, it communicates essential aspects of the approach—namely, that it is rooted in biology and dynamic systems theory, and that these systems change and evolve as does life itself.

The way people interact to form companies, the way companies interact with each other to form markets, and the way markets interact as part of the community of nation-states are all part of the biodynamic perspective. Biodynamics, by itself, is not a theory; it is an approach, a way of looking at human social behavior. It provides a unified perspective that views social behavior as participation in meaning communities, whether they are economic, national, or religious. It is a means of organizing and talking about a wide array of social phenomena.

The cornerstone of the biodynamic perspective is *Dynamic Systems Theory* (Sirkin, 1994c; see also Sirkin, 1992a, 1992b). If biodynamics is the language of organizational life, then dynamic systems theory (DST) is its grammar. DST seeks to identify the basic principles of complex adaptive systems. It is a way of looking at the world of living systems, at every level, and of predicting and understanding how those systems will behave. This is a scientific theory that seeks to explain and order a very broad range of natural phenomena.

Systems theories are not new: They have been around for more than forty years and come in a variety of shapes and sizes. DST is both a continuation of older systems theories in some ways, and a break from them in others. To appreciate the uniqueness of DST and what it has to offer, we must briefly look at the systems theories that have come before.

Systems, Systems Everywhere: Freud v. Biochemistry

The term *systems*, made popular by engineers, captures the interconnectedness and complexity of modern life. While an exhaustive, intellectual history of systems theories is beyond the scope of this book, it may be useful to acknowledge some of the more widely influential systems theories—at least those that have influenced my thinking.

Historically, there have been at least three distinct schools of systems thinking; DST is a fourth. Each school has its roots in a different tradition, uses a different language to describe its key concepts, and has given rise to a new technology or set of techniques by which its concepts can be applied to the real world.

The first school is identified with Sigmund Freud and his followers. Freud published *Group Psychology and the Analysis of the Ego* in 1921 (Freud, 1921/1955). Basing some of his ideas on the work of the French sociologist LeBon (1896/1982), Freud viewed the group as an undifferentiated mob. He emphasized regression, the loss of individuality, and the idealization of the leader as the cornerstones of his group theory. Much of the current emphasis on leadership in business writing can be traced to Freud's influence.

In the 1920s, Freud had a strong following in England that comprised two camps: ego psychology, a group that revolved around his daughter Anna; and the object relations school, which revolved around Melanie Klein. While Anna emphasized the importance of a strong ego, Klein focused on the key role of relationships. It was one of Klein's students, Wilfred Bion, who gave birth to the group psychotherapy movement (Bion, 1961).

The Kleinians emphasized the emotional impulses of the group, and often focused on the group's irrational assumptions and behavior. Bion emphasized the group-as-a-whole perspective, rather than focusing on each member's individual psychology. He identified three distinct patterns of group coping styles: dependency (on the leader), fight-flight (in relation to group members or an outside enemy), and pairing (a bonding within the group).

The followers of Bion worked out of the Tavistock Institute of Human Relations in London, and were among the first practitioners to apply group theories to organizations and work groups. These men and women, including Eric J. Miller, A. Kenneth Rice, Eric Trist, Isabel Menzies, Pierre Turquot, and Elliot Jacques, were the first psychoanalytically oriented consultants to industry. The psychoanalytically informed group movement, as it exists today, is centered at the Tavistock Institute and at the A. K. Rice Institutes in the United States. It is no longer a dominant approach to organizations, although many practitioners have been influenced by and continue to apply these ideas.

In contrast to the "soft" science approach of psychoanalysts is the "hard" science approach of physicists, chemists, and biologists. Intellectual heirs to thinkers such as Norbert Wiener and James Grier Miller, information scientists use the latest advances in theoretical physics and chemistry to understand living systems.

Beginning with mathematical studies of communication (Shannon & Weaver, 1949/1963) and early studies of cybernetics, or information feedback loops (Wiener, 1954/1963), scientists have used the key concepts of information and order to elaborate theories about complexity and chaos. This has been the stuff of serious scientific inquiry. These inquiries now constitute a body of knowledge that demonstrates the natural evolution of systems from chaotic to orderly. In 1971, Ilya Prigogine won the Nobel Prize in Chemistry for his work on far-from-equilibrium systems.

Prigogine focused on the application of the second law of thermodynamics to complex systems, including living organisms. The second law, sometimes called the law of entropy, states that physical systems tend to slide spontaneously and irreversibly toward a state of disorder. How is it, Prigogine wondered, that some systems have arisen spontaneously from less ordered states and have maintained themselves in defiance of the tendency toward entropy? Prigogine demonstrated that disordered, high-entropy systems do become more ordered and more complex over time as long as they receive energy or matter from an external source. In such situations, nonlinear systems can go through periods of instability and then self-organization, resulting in more complex systems whose characteristics cannot be predicted as a linear extrapolation from a preexisting state of affairs. They become discontinuous. They "hold" their complexity in defiance of the second law of thermodynamics (see Prigogine & Stengers, 1984).

These ideas have been popularized in the science writing of Gleick (1988) and Waldrop (1992) in their best-selling works on chaos and complexity, respectively. These ideas have been applied to business in books such as Wheatley's *Leadership and the New*

Science (1992/2001) and others.[3] The most recent developments in the field have come from members of the Santa Fe Institute, a think tank specializing in the interdisciplinary exploration of chaotic, complex systems. This community has developed a language to describe complex adaptive systems (CAS), their term for living systems. Among the most thoughtful additions to the field is the recent collection of essays aptly titled *The Biology of*

---

[3] Peter Senge (1994; Senge, Kleiner, Roberts, Ross, & Smith, 1994) deserves an honorable mention here for his best-selling series of books beginning with *The Fifth Discipline*. The eponymous discipline is, in fact, systems theory. Senge, whose version of systems thinking is couched in Sufi aphorisms, traces his intellectual lineage back to Jay Forrester. A true Renaissance man, Forrester was an electrical engineer who, after inventing the random access computer disk drive, went on to develop a version of systems thinking that he applied to industry, urban planning, and eventually the world (see Forrester, 1968). Forrester, with Senge, Norbert Wiener, and possibly the psychologist Kurt Lewin, all taught at MIT and may be lumped together as the Cambridge school of systems theory. It is a school characterized by its analytic, mathematical, even engineering focus.

I have a few reasons, maybe more properly called biases, why I don't give this school a fuller treatment in the current pages. One consideration is that there is not a fully-developed theory here. These men, although clearly influenced by each other, never represented their work as a coherent body of thought. And there are deeper problems with this approach. According to the Cambridge school, a system under discussion—be it the company, the city, or the world—is ultimately reduced to a large mechanism with innumerable inputs and outputs. The bias is toward a mechanical view, a logical-positivist conviction that seems to suggest that if only we knew all the inputs, then we could predict all the outputs. As the reader will see in the discussion of von Bertalanffy, it is the antipositivist, antireductionist emphasis of newer systems theories that I find so engaging. So does the public—which doesn't make it right but adds weight to the argument. The "butterfly effect" and other far-from-equilibrium phenomena have captured the public imagination and have liberated our thinking about cause and effect, order and chaos. My impression has always been, rightly or wrongly, that the Cambridge school, in their heart of hearts, would like nothing better than to reduce human complexity to a few well-considered mathematical formulae.

Business: Decoding the Natural Laws of Enterprise (Clippinger, 1999).

Although I have tremendous respect for this work, and believe it will bear significant fruit in the biological sciences, I have reservations about its applications to social systems. It is a body of knowledge heavily influenced by physics and chemistry. A huge theoretical leap is required to bridge the far-from-equilibrium chemical systems described by Prigogine and complex social systems. We need an intermediate theory with an intermediate language that will help us move more easily from subatomic particle physics to meaning communities.

It is precisely here that the systems theory of Ludwig von Bertalanffy, and those influenced by him, is most useful.[4]

LvB and GST

The biologist Ludwig von Bertalanffy (LvB) claimed credit as the founder of general systems theory (GST). He did much to develop and encourage the GST approach in biology, physics, and the human and social sciences. Von Bertalanffy (1968) and early GST theorists were not exactly modest in their claims, and their enthusiasm approached religious zeal. As with many new movements, whether in politics or science, these systems theorists stressed their differences with the mainstream (see Koestler, 1978) and saw themselves as pioneers. They were invested in their

---

[4] It's necessary to note that von Bertalanffy was a member of the Nazi Party, in connection with his teaching position at the University of Vienna, from 1938–1945. This has, of course, complicated his legacy. See Drack, Manfred; Apfalter, Wilfried; Pouvreau, David (11 March 2017). "On the Making of a System Theory of Life: Paul A Weiss and Ludwig von Bertalanffy's Conceptual Connection". *The Quarterly review of biology.* pp. 349–373.

self-image as explorers of a completely new approach that allowed them to see what others had missed.

Mark Twain said that only Adam could claim originality with any assurance. Thus it is that we can trace the roots of general systems theory to the German *Naturphilosophie of* the eighteenth and nineteenth centuries, exemplified by Hegel and Goethe, and to the vitalists who trace their origins to Aristotle. All of these approaches share the conviction that certain natural phenomena, typically those associated with life, are unique and unaccountably complex. They are fundamentally different from and irreducible to the nonliving world of matter. In this view, sometimes referred to as *holism*, a contrast is made between the physical, nonliving world and the world of animate nature.

The first, nonliving world is best seen as a mechanism or giant machine, analyzable according to physical laws. The second, living world has laws of its own that, while not contradicting those of physics, are also not fully reducible to them. The work of Prigogine and others in the chaos sciences has done much to expose this as a false dichotomy.

In light of recent developments, von Bertalanffy may seem a bit dated. However, the view that living systems are discontinuous, i.e., far from equilibrium, is still a cornerstone of the "new science." Unlike the other schools of systems theory discussed above, von Bertalanffy's school is grounded in principles thoroughly consistent with biological phenomena. This put him in a position to influence people whom the other systems theories could never reach.

"The whole is greater than the sum of its parts." This is the great catchphrase of general systems theory, its alpha and omega, its first incisive insight and its final ringing truth. While some may

find this observation trivially obvious, GST theorists found it profound, even revolutionary. Among other things, it tells us that all the analysis in the world, all the breaking down into smaller and smaller elementary particles, will still leave us missing something essential. Analysis, no matter how thorough, will always be insufficient. It is the program of general systems theory to provide thorough explanations by attending to the "complexes of elements standing in interaction" (von Bertalanffy, 1968, p. 33) and not simply to the elements themselves.

The interaction, in all its patterned complexity, is more interesting for the systems thinker than an analysis of the elements that constitute the system.

For better or worse, and from an early stage, von Bertalanffy was self-consciously creating an alternative science. The very term "general systems theory" was carefully chosen to mirror Einstein's general theory of relativity. Perhaps more important than the ideas themselves, von Bertalanffy created the social structures to carry forward his program. He used meetings of the American Association for the Advancement of Science to recruit and proselytize. He created the Society for General Systems Research, and encouraged publications in a wide range of areas. He also saw the founding of the Center for Advanced Study in the Behavioral Sciences in Palo Alto, near Stanford (again a parallel to Einstein's home base in Princeton), which became a think tank that explored the many ramifications of a broadly applied general systems theory.

From Palo Alto, the first inklings of an applied discipline of systems theory in the social sciences began to emerge. It was Gregory Bateson, resident Renaissance man, who gathered a group that eventually gave birth to the applied systems discipline known as *family therapy*.

Bateson was the author of seminal works in the area that I am calling applied systems theory. The very title of his most enduring work, a set of essays entitled *Steps to an Ecology of Mind: Collected Essays in Anthropology, Psychiatry, Evolution, and Epistemology* (Bateson, 1972) suggests the breadth and scope of his thinking.

As a systems thinker who was both subtle and profound, Bateson was able to weave the connecting threads among communications theory, sociology, anthropology, biology, and ecology. But perhaps even more seminal than his own writings was his influence on his group. His students and colleagues permanently altered the psychotherapy landscape.

At the Mental Research Institute, people like Jay Haley, Paul Watzlowick, Virginia Satir, and others created a therapeutic movement based on the power of words and communication to shape the experience of reality. This movement eventually grew into the many schools of family therapy, and also offshoots that encompassed everything from the therapeutic use of metaphor in hypnosis (Haley, 1973) to neurolinguistic programming (Bandler & Grinder, 1975). Some of their ideas on the reality-shaping power of metaphors and narrative are again becoming popular in the literature on corporate storytelling (see Denning, 2001).

Bateson and his colleagues' wide-ranging application of systems theory gave a powerful boost to the previous, more staid versions of systems theory. The community of meaning that arises from shared language and interactions actually creates a worldview that is both symbolic and quite real. A worldview created through multiple conversations over time exists as an emergent property of language communities, or what I have called meaning communities. The shared meanings and symbols that cohere in a community over time shape the experience of its members. This is what we call *culture*. Sociologists refer to this emergent quality as *symbolic interactionism*. The inhabitants of the fourth kingdom are, thus, symbolically interactive meaning communities.

The Need for a New Systems Theory

Kurt Lewin said, "There is nothing quite so practical as a good theory." There is a virtual Tower of Babel when it comes to systems theory or schools of systems theory. I have identified at least four in these pages, and perhaps several more depending on how one groups various writers. Within each school, there are potential offshoots and subschools. The following chart may be helpful:

Table 1
Schools of Systems Thought

School	Founder	Advantages	Disadvantages
Psychodynamic (PDS)	Sigmund Freud	• Simple • Psychological	• Simplistic • Nonscalable
System Dynamics (SD)	Jay Forrester	• Complex • Technically adequate	• Too mechanical • Diffuse
General Systems Theory (GST)	Ludwig von Bertalanffy	• Biological • Social	• Nonanalytic • Too global
Complex Adaptive Systems (CAS)	Ilya Prigogine	• Cutting-edge science • Continuity between physics and biology	• Too many elements • Not systematic

One of the primary reasons for this cacophony of ideas is that each founder comes from a different discipline, speaks a different technical language, and arrives at his theory, in part, to answer a separate set of technical challenges. It is a testament to the robustness of the phenomena under consideration that all of these disparate ideas can have such striking similarities and go under the general rubric of systems theory.

"Why in the world," you may well ask, "do we need yet *another* systems theory?" Or to approach it another way, what should a new systems theory offer to make its inclusion useful?

In the first place, and at the very least, a new theory should not retain any of the disadvantages that hamper previous theories. That is, a new systems theory should not:

- Be too simplistic
- Be too mechanistic
- Try to be all things to all people
- View everything as a system (or else systems *per se* are no longer meaningful)
- On the other hand, a new systems theory should:
- Be amenable to analysis
- Be scalable—meaning it accommodates large and small systems equally well
- Reduce the number of phenomena under consideration rather than multiply them
- Be, where possible, a systematic and coherent body of principles

At the same time, a new systems theory should retain as many of the advantages of as many of the schools as possible:

- Simple without being simplistic
- Consistent with the latest scientific knowledge
- Complex enough to handle a wide variety of phenomena
- Able to shed light upon technical issues in areas in the hard and soft sciences

Dynamic systems theory meets most, if not all, of these challenges. It is an approach to systems that can be boiled down to seven essential principles or axioms. Each axiom represents a universal aspect of systems. The theory is designed to be scalable, at least in terms of living systems. That is, it is appropriate for biological organisms as small as a bacterium and as large as planet Earth, and everything in between.

Unlike the other systems theories, DST was designed with the others in mind, in order to capture the strengths of all without falling prey to the vulnerabilities of each. Ultimately the goal of DST is to capture the fluid, changing nature of systems that are *alive*.[5]

One additional advantage of DST is worth mentioning. While each of the four other systems theories evolved from a particular discipline, DST is a conscious amalgam of several disciplines. It derives from, and is meant to be useful for, a variety of applied social science venues, from psychotherapy to social psychology to organizational consulting.

---

[5] DST, as any theory, will have to compete with other system theories for goodness of fit. As the CAS theorists would say, it must traverse a fitness landscape to demonstrate its ability to meet the specific challenges required by those using such theories. Ultimately these theories are a tool, and their utility determines their survival; their adaptability and robustness will determine their fitness.

The issue of consilience is a relevant consideration at this point. Consilience refers to a growing tendency for scientific theories from various fields to converge and complement each other (Wilson, 1998). As physics converges with chemistry, which converges with biology, and so on, we are coming closer and closer to a theory of everything. Consistently missing from these efforts, in my opinion, is a linking of individual psychology with sociology with economics with political theory—areas that have historically been neglected by other systems theories. I would suggest that DST and the biodynamic approach, as elaborated in the following pages, may begin to fill this need.

Management at the Crossroads

For all the paper and profits that business publishers generate—the innumerable books, articles, and magazines on everything from leadership to money management—these writings are woefully lacking in any grounding deeper than their own self-reference. I can count on one hand the number of business philosophers who are currently contributing to the field, primarily Charles Handy and Peter Drucker, to cite the two best-known examples.

The practice of business is too significant, the work of managers too important, not to try to connect them to some of the other great ideas of the recent past. DST and biodynamics at least permit us to begin the work of connecting management theory to physics, biology, psychology, and sociology.

The truth is that there is no unified approach to management. As a management consultant, part of my job is to stay abreast of the latest trends and ideas that impact managers and corporations. *Fad Surfing in the Boardroom,* the title of one book has called it (Shapiro, 1995). The approaches come fast and furious: reengineering, the balanced scorecard, Six Sigma, and more. Add to these other popular titles, such as *Jesus CEO, Moses on Management, Elizabeth I CEO,* and the perennial favorite, *Management Secrets of Attila the Hun,* and one catches a hint of the confusion.

I have nothing against any of these views and find them all useful in their own way. But the very existence of so many disparate approaches indicates a lack of agreement, if not downright bewilderment. In the face of such cacophony, perhaps the best course of action is silence. And yet …

The Fourth Kingdom Beckons

I believe we are poised at an historical moment—not just in human history, but also for the history of life on the planet. Corporations, appearing a mere few hundred years ago on the world scene, have quickly become the most vital force, the most dominant life form on earth. The organizational form is currently undergoing an explosion unlike anything since the Cambrian era, half a billion years ago. This continuity, from the first animals to the most recent internet company, is the story of the evolution of life on the planet.

The interaction of humans with their technological tools is creating entirely new ways of exploiting economic and planetary resources. Can the exploitation of interplanetary resources be far behind? Mankind, through its participation in these corporate actualities, is morphing into something unknown before in the universe. It is not the end of man, but it is the beginning of something new, something metahuman.

Just as the first multicelled organism was not the end of unicellular life, man will live side by side with the corporations that emerge from his economic efforts. Our temporal perspective here is thousands, if not hundreds of thousands, of years—a far cry from the quarter-to-quarter time horizon of most managers and CEOs.

2

THE BUILDING BLOCKS OF A BIODYNAMIC THEORY

*I*n this chapter, I introduce the reader to a set of principles, in the form of seven axioms that lie at the heart of all living systems, including organizations. The emergent principle, Axiom 1, illustrates the importance of levels and the philosophy of emergence when trying to understand complex systems. The integral principle, Axiom 2, emphasizes the importance of boundaries in healthy systems. The differentiation principle, Axiom 3, shows how and why systems become increasingly complex. Axiom 4, the principle of hierarchy, illustrates how systems maximize efficiency and coordination through leading parts. Axiom 5 introduces the development principle, which states that systems can grow in an orderly and predictable fashion over time. Axiom 6 discusses how systems make use of energy for individual, and population, growth; this is the autopoietic principle. The synthetic principle, Axiom 7,

recognizes that systems combine in essentially unpredictable ways
that reflect a natural chaos and thwart simple, linear predictability.[1]

Essential Elements of Dynamic Systems

What do all systems have in common?

If we look at this from the broadest possible perspective, the first
and most notable aspect of systems is simply how many of them
there are. Not just thousands or millions or billions, not just a
google or a googolplex, but *everything* is systems. And not just
a single system, but systems within systems within systems, *ad
infinitum.*

The number of systems in the world is countless. Yet science
teaches us that there is an order to these systems. This order
has been graphically represented in the new Rose Center in
the American Museum of Natural History in New York City.
Beginning at the top of a four-story sphere, the visitor walks down
a ramp that starts with the largest known thing, the universe
itself, estimated at a size of 10^{26} (using the size of a person as the
benchmark, or 10 to the first power). As the visitor proceeds down
the ramp, objects or distances are described in descending order,
from largest to smallest, as far down as 10^{-15}. And at every level,
as far as we know, there are systems.

---

[1] This chapter and the next present rather technical and philosophical
discussions of the axioms of dynamic systems theory. Any scholar of systems
theory, or anyone hoping to master the intricacies of the application of DST
to a variety of phenomena, will need to fully understand these chapters.
For others, especially those who are looking simply to apply these ideas to a
business setting, these chapters can be passed over. Read carefully the axioms
themselves (at the end of this chapter), and feel free to refer back to these pages
if the need arises.

The *levels* of systems must be where we begin in any discussion of a systems view of the world. Systems do not exist in isolation, but in a vast interconnection of systems within systems on top of systems. The levels emerge from each other; every system is a by-product of an aggregate of systems at a level below. To fully understand any system requires an understanding of the levels between which it is sandwiched. *Boundaries* create a system, define a system, and determine what the system is and is not. Everything inside the boundary is part of the identity of the system, while the area outside the boundary is extrasystemic. Boundaries are the *sine qua non* of systems—necessary if not sufficient.

Differentiation is the key to fitness adaptation. It allows systems to specialize, to develop components that permit the whole system to adapt to the environment. At the same time, differentiation provides for specialization within the system. I call differentiation "the secret genius of organizations."

Hierarchy, or leadership, is the means by which systems coordinate their activity. Some feminists and socialists believe that these are not abiding principles of systems but leftover biases of a male, class-oriented society. While I agree that it is difficult to overestimate the bias that our own social systems create in us, there is still a principle of systems here that goes well beyond our own social structures. All systems seem to have lead components. In insect societies, as the queen goes, so goes the hive. Leadership in our society is not just a current obsession; it has been an important issue throughout recorded time, including when we choose female or proletariat leaders. Even at the cellular level, we see nuclei organizing the activity of cells.

Systems have a life cycle, a path of *development* that is predictable. By studying the developmental patterns of any system, scientists and practitioners can begin to differentiate healthy development from unhealthy development, the expected from the unexpected. It is the cornerstone of natural history and the beginning of science.

Growth, the way systems expand over time, requires interaction with the environment. Growth demands the crossing of boundaries and implies interaction and exchange between systems. Despite the equilibrium tendencies of systems, there is nevertheless one undeniable fact: Systems change, they morph, they become something other than what they were. This growth requires energy and the utilization of resources. Moreover, it is fundamentally unpredictable.

Chaos, if not the ultimate arbiter, is certainly a loud and constant voice in the choir of change. It is not that cause and effect are not operative; they certainly are. It is that predictability is more hope than reality in the natural world of systems.

Levels, boundaries, differentiation, and hierarchy are the essential characteristics of any system, the elemental qualities that must be articulated to understand the system as it exists. In DST, we refer to these as *axioms of structure.*

Development, growth, and chaos are aspects of the system that refer to its interactions, both with the elements that comprise it and with the elements and systems with which it interacts. In DST, these are referred to as *axioms of process.*

The remainder of this chapter examines each of these characteristics in depth.

Level upon Level

The emergent properties of systems give them their life. Yet the very fact of emergence is where we must begin to lay the foundations of a viable and inclusive systems theory. The fact of emergence leads us to the first axiom:

> *Axiom 1:* Nature is organized in levels such that each level comprises a number of elements that, taken together, form an element of the next level.

This is to say, at any level, the basic units that comprise that level combine in the next level up to become the elements of that next level, and so on. Particles combine into atoms, atoms into molecules, molecules into cells, cells into organs, organs into people, people into families, families into communities, communities into nations, and nations into the world—and back down again. The idea of levels, their multiplicity, and their interconnectedness is an essential aspect of dynamic systems theory. It is not possible to fully comprehend any element without taking into account the level above it and the level below. (See Figure 2-1.)

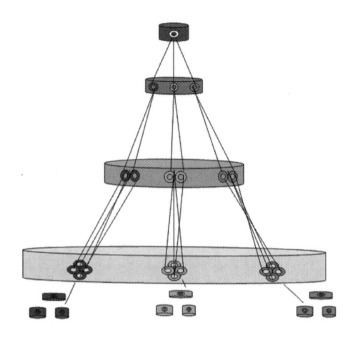

Figure 2-1—The Emergent Levels of Systems

Arthur Koestler (1978) referred to this dual aspect of systems as *the Janus principle*. Janus was the Roman god of gates and doors and was represented as having two faces, one looking in and one looking out. Koestler suggested a general term, *holon*, for the elements in a system:

> ... a new term to designate those Janus-faced entities on the intermediate levels of any hierarchy, which can be described either as wholes or as parts, depending on the way you look at them from 'below' or from 'above.' The term [he] propose[d] was the '*holon*,' from the Greek **holos** = whole, with suffix **on**, which as in proton or neutron, suggests a particle or part. (Koestler, 1978, p. 33)

A holon is any particle that can be appreciated in its dual aspect as both an entity unto itself and as a component in a larger whole. As an entity, we may say that a holon exhibits emergent properties that are not obvious in its constitutive elements. Brain cells, to return to our earlier example, are holons that exhibit certain biochemical properties when viewed from "below" or analytically. When viewed from "above" as an orchestrated whole, these cells work together to exhibit this wonderful quality we call "mind," a quality that seems not to be wholly contained in any brain cell or brain region.

As a corollary of the Janus principle, Koestler suggested that all holons have two complementary dynamic potential tendencies: "an *integrative tendency* to function as part of the larger whole, and a *self-assertive tendency* to preserve its individual autonomy" (Koestler, 1978, p. 57). So when a holon is part of a larger system, functioning in some coordinated way with other holons, we may say that its integrative tendency is dominant. When, however, the holon exists in relative isolation, we may say that its self- assertive tendency is dominant.

Ideas such as "integrative tendency" and "self-assertive tendency" are seductive, especially in discussions about human systems, but are ultimately of questionable value, particularly as explanatory principles. A person can say on one occasion, "I am for myself in this case; I don't care about the others," and in another instance say, "I'll forego my self-interest for the sake of the others." While these statements may be clear examples of the self-assertive tendency and the integrative tendency respectively, these ideas become problematic beyond the human realm. What sense does it make for the entomologist to ask, "Does the honeybee graze flowers for herself or for the hive?"

These questions are problematic on higher levels as well: Does the sick employee come to work for herself or for the company? Does a soldier fight for personal honor and survival or for the greater good? Koestler's tendencies may only make sense from the viewpoint of an outside observer, as a convention of description of an individual element within a larger system. In other words, integrative tendencies and self-assertive tendencies are not actual properties within a member of a system, but rather are useful ways to describe a dual tension or pull within all members of all systems. It is never a case of either/or, but simply the salience of one or the other at any given point in time.

This duality, and the struggle with it, may sound familiar. It goes beyond Koestler's terminology because it reflects an age-old debate in biology, ethology, and psychology. It also cuts across two of the thorniest problems in psychology: the mind-body problem and the nature-nurture controversy.

The problem may be posed this way: Do people make decisions independently—are they free agents—or are they compelled to do the things they do by their biological makeup? Asked this way, with the implication that either one or the other is true and therefore the alternative is false, the questions are unanswerable.

I recently challenged a colleague to tell me one important thing that psychology has discovered in its one hundred years as a science. After a brief pause, he said thoughtfully, "Well, we know that we are 50% nature and 50% nurture" (although I wasn't sure, it seemed his tongue was caught in his cheek at the time). The truth of the matter is we are 100% nature and 100% nurture, because the reality does not cleave as neatly as the question implies. Similarly with the mind-body problem, as discussed above, it seems much more satisfactory to conceptualize mind as an emergent property of brain, inextricably linking the two, than to choose one mode of explanation over another.

Some ethologists and Freudians still find terms such as "instinct" useful in describing animals and man. In fact, Koestler tries to make the case that his integrative tendency is identical to Freud's Eros while his self-assertive tendency corresponds to Freud's Thanatos (Koestler, 1978, pp. 57–69). Such general terms for phenomena as wide-ranging as death, war, independence, and aggression are problematic. Certainly, at least in the case of Freud, the agenda of reducing complex phenomena to straightforward expressions of instinct is evident. Although Koestler is an avowed anti-reductionist, it seems he is nevertheless willing to succumb to the temptation of an all-encompassing principle or first cause. When asked to describe an instinct, Gregory Bateson (1972) replied that it was "an explanatory principle." When asked what it explained, he replied, "Anything—almost anything at all. Anything you want it to explain" (p. 38).

Herein lies the problem with instinct and with Koestler's tendencies. In this sense, they are like our axioms. They are not final explanations but may perhaps serve as way stations, an agreement to stop digging the foundation so we can get on with building the edifice.

Structural Solutions to Vital Problems

The first axiom, which deals with the phenomena of emergence, tells us that life is organized in levels. Each level exhibits certain characteristics that are qualitatively different from the preceding level, which is to say that each level has integrity in relation to the levels above and below; it is a part, yet apart.

For example, a cell has its own discrete structure even though it is a component in tissue, which is a component in an organ, and so on. We cannot speak of life without speaking of structure, and the story of evolution is the story of the evolution of structure in nature. We can identify a trend from undifferentiated wholes to increasingly complex levels of differentiation and order. With some important caveats (see Gould, 1989), we can identify this trend both ontogenetically, in the life of the individual, and phylogenetically, in the history of life. It is this spectrum of differentiation that our next several axioms will address.

To Be or Not to Be

Axiom 2: **Any viable system can and must function as an integral whole at some point in its life cycle, despite its ultimate refractability or summativity.**

This axiom, which represents the *integral principle*, tells us that a system must in some sense be able to stand on its own. A boundary of some sort is the most common indicator of a system's integrity.

While the first axiom was concerned with the existence of multiple levels, the second axiom is concerned primarily with a single level. It recognizes that, at a given level, there are pluralities of elements that together constitute a given system. This is sometimes referred to as the *summative principle* in general systems theory (von Bertalanffy, 1968). If a system can be minimally defined as "a set of elements standing in interrelation," then in this second axiom we have the barest essentials of a system. The multiplicity of elements and their functional relationship are the two essential features of a viable system.

Even though we may be able to divide a system into its elements, and those elements into smaller elements, the system or entity or unit must be a whole in some meaningful way. This susceptibility to division refers to the system's ultimate *refractability*. This refractability, the quality that allows systems to be analyzed, is the first corollary of Axiom 2.

On the other hand, the integrity of a system must hold even if the units combine to form a suprasystem, or coherent level of organization at one or more levels up. That is, the simple system, even though it is an element in the larger system, must still be capable of being a whole by itself. This latter quality corresponds to the *summativity* of elements within a given system and represents the second corollary of the second axiom.

Vive les Différences

Systems only really get interesting when we realize that all the parts within a given system are not equal. When we study the human body as a collection of organ systems, for example, the fact that each organ is different and has a specialized purpose in terms of the whole body is inspiring. It was this complex coordination of parts in living things, and the way these living things coordinated with each other in nature, that convinced Kant that God existed and created the world in a purposeful way (the teleological argument for God).

Axiom 3: **Systems tend to become increasingly complex and to differentiate their parts such that each performs different functions in the service of the whole.**

Let us refer to this third axiom as the *differentiation principle*. Simply put, simple systems don't stay simple; their parts tend to become specialized over time, each performing more or less different functions in complex interrelationship. As the system becomes more complex, subsystems may form. A subsystem may consist of components that are different in function or structure from other components of the system. Implicit in this notion is the idea of *progressive segregation* (von Bertalanffy, 1968).

A system begins as an undifferentiated whole, with parts that are relatively uniform and interchangeable. As the system functions in its environment, different parts begin to perform different functions. These differences may arise from necessity or convenience, from accidents of location or chance structural variations. However these differences arise, they become functional and therefore are maintained structurally in the system. Where there was once an undifferentiated whole, there are parts, and where there was once a uniformity of parts, there are specialized parts that perform specific functions.

As a crude example, imagine the formation of a boundary structure—a skin or cell membrane, for instance. Initially the outer layer is not differentiable from the inside. Over time, though, an outer layer forms, one that may serve to contain the inner layers or prevent unregulated interaction with the outside. The membrane is then a structure that has been segregated and differentiated from the rest of the system; it is part of and apart from the system.

This tendency toward complexity does not arise mysteriously. It is a function of segregation and differentiation. In the language of systems theory, living systems are open systems and must therefore manage influxes of energy to survive. In closed systems, energy tends to run down, to disperse from areas of concentration to emptier regions, leading to a uniform distribution throughout the universe. This is the second law of thermodynamics, known as *entropy*.

A decrease in entropy is negative entropy, or *negentropy*. Living systems have the unique ability to counteract entropy, to store energy and prevent, albeit briefly sometimes, the increase in overall entropy that is the fate of the universe. Open or living systems, if they can transport energy in, can use stored energy to maintain their functioning for a period of time.

We will return to these important considerations when we discuss how systems use energy. For now, let us simply acknowledge that segregation in living systems serves to keep energy in the system and inhibit its dissipation. Segregation counteracts entropy.

As differentiation continues, progressive segregation leads to *progressive mechanization* (von Bertalanffy, 1968). The segregated parts specialize and begin to function autonomously, independent from the whole. The system develops specialized subsystems that perform functions more precisely and more efficiently than the whole, but with less flexibility.

What the overall system loses because parts are no longer interchangeable, it makes up for with increased efficiency. It is difficult to overestimate the importance of progressive mechanization in living systems; it is a necessary condition of progressive evolution and structural change.

To illustrate the importance of specialized subsystems, or progressive mechanization, Herbert Simon (1960) tells the following allegory:

> Once there were two watchmakers, Tempus and Hora. Both were famous for the watches they made, marvelously complex timepieces each consisting of 1000 working parts. And while the watches were roughly equivalent in quality,

function, and price, Hora prospered while Tempus could not survive. The only difference between the two lay in the process by which they built their watches. Tempus assembled each of his thousand pieces sequentially, one after the other, and if he was interrupted for any reason and had to lay down his work, the entire job fell apart and he had to start over again from the beginning. Hora, on the other hand, assembled his watches by using small subassemblies of ten parts each. So ten small subassemblies of ten parts each were assembled to create a larger subassembly of 100 parts, ten of which were combined to create a whole thousand piece watch. If Hora was interrupted he had to reassemble the subassembly he was working on but the other subassemblies remained intact.

If the two methods seem only trivially different, think again. Assume that there is one chance in a hundred that the watchmakers will be interrupted in their work. This means it will take Tempus 4,000 times as long to assemble a watch as it takes Hora. Hora's method, which corresponds to progressive mechanization, is significantly more robust and ultimately more successful.

Adam Smith, the Scottish economist, recognized as early as 1776 the utility of progressive mechanization in the factory. Using his example of a pin manufacturer, he demonstrated that several individuals, each specializing in a different aspect of pin making, could together produce many more pins than the same number of individuals each making entire pins from start to finish. From subcellular structures to multinational corporations, progressive mechanization is a strategy that works.

Yet progressive mechanization does come with a cost. In a primal system, all elements are equipotential—that is, any element can do the job of any other element. Henry Ford built the first automobile single-handedly. By the time of his death, automobiles were built on assembly lines in which each worker could perform only a small fraction of the many steps needed to produce one automobile. No doubt the assembly line produced each car faster and cheaper, but any given worker had much less flexibility (in knowledge, resources, and craftsmanship) than the original Ford.

The same phenomenon can be seen in insect societies where individuals develop into highly specialized members of a caste. No individual of the hive is capable of independent survival. In exchange for efficiency, the "complexified" system trades in its equipotential parts for highly specialized ones.

This exchange is usually beneficial, but the cost is a significant reduction in flexibility. In times of crisis, this may threaten the system's survival. This is a dilemma with which many organizations struggle as they move from entrepreneurial status to a more mature organizational form.

Following the Leader

Closely related to the idea of complexity is the manner of organization that invariably takes place in complex systems. This leads to the fourth systems axiom, the *hierarchical principle*.

Axiom 4: **The components of complex systems will tend to organize around leading parts, thus producing hierarchical structures in systems.**

Leading structures, central structures, and hierarchical order are related ideas that convey a characteristic common in the organization of living systems. In most cases, the central structure is obvious, as in the nucleus of a cell or the chief of a tribe. These leading parts tend to be primary in terms of both function and time: They are usually the first structures in systems, and often serve regulating or control functions.

Many systems thinkers hold that hierarchical organization is the given of a system, and that elements without this type of organization hardly warrant being called systems (see von Bertalanffy, Koestler). The centrality of hierarchy is not only an obvious organizing principle for those who think about systems, but an empirical reality as well. Simon (1960), who gave us the Tempus and Hora allegory, has stated:

> Complex systems will evolve from simple systems much more rapidly if there are stable intermediate forms than if there are not. The resulting complex forms in the former case will be hierarchic. We have only to turn the argument round to explain the observed predominance of hierarchies among the complex systems Nature presents to us. Among possible complex forms, hierarchies are the ones that had the time to evolve.

Simon not only stresses the importance of hierarchical organization in the evolution of living systems, but also shows how closely tied are the phenomena of complexity, progressive mechanization, and hierarchical organization.

There is a sense, however, in which leadership or centrality is relative and not always so clear. Paul Weiss must have been sensitive to just such a criticism when he said, perhaps a bit defensively, "The phenomenon of hierarchic structure is a real one, presented to us by the biological object, and not the fiction of a speculative mind" (as cited in Koestler & Smythies, 1969).

While leadership or centrality is often a very useful tool for the systems analyst, from within a system, such terms as leader/follower, top/bottom, or center/periphery are often relative. For example, in a corporate hierarchy, one often finds a chairman of the board, a CEO, a president, and an executive vice president. Each is a leader in some sense, and *the* leader in some contexts. Yet not one of them is fully in control at every point in time.

The queen bee is the leader of her hive until she can no longer fulfill that function, at which time the workers do what is necessary to create a new queen. Queen bees or ants are often giant egg-laying matriarchs more enslaved by their roles than any worker could be.

Perspective is an important consideration in determining leadership roles. In the early part of the century, ethologists who observed primate behavior felt that they could easily discern the social structure of primate groups. In most cases, observers saw large, older males as being in charge, with females and younger group members taking subordinate positions. More recent studies have demonstrated that these early observations were hopelessly biased and that dominance patterns are much more complex and fluid. The early observers interpreted social structure based on their prejudices. A leading part from one perspective may be a subordinate component from another.

Differentiation often leads to hierarchy, and the two aspects of a system may be earlier and later manifestations of the same underlying process. Here we begin to see the very tight coupling of Axiom 3 with Axiom 4. As elements begin to differentiate and specialize, one of the earliest types of specialization that seems to occur is a control element that becomes a central structure.

This inevitably leads to the hierarchies observed by many systems analysts.

The importance of central structures is debatable. Von Bertalanffy (1968) refers repeatedly to the principle of centralization and states that "an 'individual' can be defined as a centralized system" (p. 71). In his version of systems theory, "progressive centralization constitutes progressive individualization."

Other systems theorists (see Koestler) seem not to need the concept of centralization at all.

There are two significant problems with centralization as von Bertalanffy defines it. The first is the problem of perspective, and the second is the problem of hierarchies in relation to centered individuals.

In terms of perspective, all of the problems that I identified with the relativity of leading parts apply to centered individuals. The question is simply, which elements in a given system are central and which are peripheral?

Leadership may be obvious or it may be subtle. Control may seem centralized at one point, but may be dependent on various events at other points. Or control may be passed from one element of the system to another, depending on circumstance. To the extent that we can decide this question of centrality independently of perspective, this concept will be useful in describing systems. However, as discussed above, this is not always a simple or obvious matter. It may not be possible to disengage the question from the relativity of perspective.

Centralization is also problematic from the standpoint of hierarchies. No sooner is a system specified in terms of its center than attention to its hierarchical nature will lead us away from the center. The perspective from the center is often at odds with a hierarchical view of the same system. It may be tempting to think of the top of the hierarchy as equivalent to the central, controlling structures of a system, but again, this is dependent on perspective.

When discussing General Motors, one might focus on the chairman of the board (i.e., hierarchies), while in discussions of cell structure, one might focus on nuclei (i.e., central structures). It seems that as systems analysts, we can choose to focus on centers or focus on hierarchies, but not both.

I have chosen, in the fourth axiom, to focus on hierarchies. The idea of centeredness is important and will be discussed below in terms of autonomy, but it shall not be granted axiomatic status in the present version of DST.

Although in Axiom 1, the multilayered quality of systems was discussed, we are now in a position to talk about these layers in more detail. The levels mentioned in Axiom 1 are not always clear-cut. There is not always an undisputed demarcation where one level ends and another begins. The reason for this is that as differentiation occurs, there is a subtle but progressive loss of equipotentiality. As some structures become unable to perform some functions, a growing dependence or interdependence of elements emerges.

On a given level, this entails the emergence of lead parts and the development of hierarchies, as we have discussed. However, the process that creates hierarchies *within* a given level also seems to function *between* levels. Control structures within a level lead to levels of control between levels.

For example, in simple organisms, nervous tissue is responsible for conducting electrical impulses within the body. As these simple organisms evolved into more complex organisms, nervous tissue became the nervous system, which controls and coordinates interactions among functionally related organ and tissue groups. The system evolved a brain, and it is the brain, for the most part, that speaks to other brains in the system we call society.

Control structures are not imposed on a system, but rather emerge gradually and organically from the system. These control structures, in essence, are put forth by the system for the sake of the system, to control the system by coordinating its function with other parts of the system. From an outside perspective, what began as subtle differentiation becomes permanently cast in hierarchical structure.

The Processes of Systems in Time

Early systems theorists tended to focus on structure and ignore the complications posed by time. It wasn't that they were unaware of these problems; they simply felt they had solved them.

To put systems theory in an historical context, it is important to understand how earlier scientists dealt with time. Alvin Toffler, in his foreword to Prigogine and Stengers's book *Order Out of Chaos* (1984), reviews this history:

> In the world model constructed by Newton and his followers, time was an afterthought. A moment, whether in the present, past, or future, was assumed to be exactly like any other moment. In classical or mechanistic science, events begin with 'initial conditions,' and their atoms or particles follow 'world lines' or trajectories. These

can be traced either backward into the past or forward into the future. ... For this reason, scientists refer to time in Newtonian systems as 'reversible.'

In the nineteenth century, however, as the main focus of physics shifted from dynamics to thermodynamics and the Second Law of thermodynamics was proclaimed, time suddenly became a central concern. For, according to the Second Law, there is an inescapable loss of energy in the universe. And, if the world machine is really running down and approaching the heat death, then it follows that one moment is no longer exactly like the last. You cannot run the universe backward to make up for entropy. Events over the long term cannot replay themselves. And this means that there is a directionality or, as Eddington later called it, an 'arrow' in time. (pp. xix–xx)

The early systems theorists were not ignorant of these considerations; far from it. It was the second law of thermodynamics that made life so paradoxical. The challenge they set before themselves was to make the life sciences consistent with the second law. The solution was to create a distinction between *closed systems*, which move inexorably toward entropic equilibrium, and *open systems*, which can transport energy and information across the boundary and maintain organization, seemingly in spite of the second law. Open systems—that is, living systems—are negentropic; they conserve energy, in the form of information, and thereby counteract entropy.

So the problem of time was largely ignored in early systems theory because it was thought to have been explained away. Time was only a problem in closed systems that lost energy due to entropy. This led to a de-emphasis on time-related problems and processes and a corresponding emphasis on structure, i.e., the timeless and enduring aspects of a system. For the early systems theorists, structure was destiny.

This is why the first four axioms of DST are *axioms of structure*. The axioms to follow, I call *axioms of process*, because they each deal with changes in systems over time.

Individual Systems: Islands in Time

As we have seen, systems are not static. In Axiom 2, I referred to the life cycle of the system. In Axiom 5, I will make this life cycle explicit.

> *Axiom 5*: Over time, systems change in regular and predictable ways during the course of their life cycles.

Axiom 5 is the *developmental principle*. The tendency to differentiate implies the existence of a process over time—a developmental process.

The developmental process in living things, and often by analogy in nonliving things, may be thought of in terms of a life cycle. All living things may be described in these terms: They are born, they grow, they mature, and they die. People and other individual creatures have such life cycles. So do communities, cultures, nations, and civilizations. So do stars and galaxies, business corporations and bureaucracies.

All systems exhibit regular patterns of functioning over time, with specific patterns associated in a specific sequence during the life of the system.

The unique developmental course of an organism is usually referred to as *ontogeny*, a term that conveys the sense of development of being. To the classical mind, however, being simply *is*—it is a thing's essence. As in Aristotle's conception of causality, to speak of a thing developing could only mean that it was becoming more of what it really was: Children were small adults, and seeds were immature trees.

The modern mind, on the other hand, easily accepts the idea of sequential developmental stages, of the transformations that occur naturally over time. A caterpillar is not simply a larval form, but a being with unique patterns of functioning and rules specific to its developmental stage. That it may become a butterfly is not irrelevant, but neither is that fact its essential, defining characteristic.

The notion of development introduces the element of time into our discussion of systems.

A Time to Every Purpose: The Replication of Structure in Time

Any comprehensive discussion of systems must acknowledge the fact that living systems have the potential to grow and reproduce. It is this property more than any other that makes systems so dynamic. Indeed, words like *vital* and *vivacious*, derived from the Latin word for "life," are synonymous with the robust energy associated with healthy living systems. A technical term for the ability of a system to replicate itself is *autopoiesis*, from the Greek words *auto* (self), and *poiesis* (to create) (Maturana & Varela, 1987). The *autopoietic principle* is the sixth axiom:

> *Axiom 6*: Living systems have the ability to self-replicate by extracting raw materials from their environments and incorporating these materials for purposes of system maintenance and propagation.

It is difficult to imagine a living system that does not have the potential for self-replication. The prototypical example is that of the amoeba, a free-living unicellular creature that takes in complex compounds across the cell membrane and self-replicates by dividing into two unicellular creatures that are nearly exact replicas of the original. The law of entropy is circumvented by the ability of these open systems to take in materials across the boundary. If the amoeba, or any other living thing, were a closed system, it would run down. Because it is an open system, it has the ability to transform raw materials and thereby grow.

Growth can be understood in two ways: as it pertains to the individual organism, and as it pertains to a population of organisms. Both are consequences of autopoietic processes, but their effects are manifested at different system levels. Individuals grow and populations grow, and each process is different enough to require a separate corollary.

The *first corollary* pertains to the growth of individual systems, and it states: *Through transportation-transformation processes, a system is capable of sustaining and augmenting its functions throughout its life cycle.* Transportation-transformation processes refer to boundaries, the transport of raw materials across a boundary, and the transmutation of this material into organismic components within the boundary.

Arguably, this corollary belongs to Axiom 5 because it refers to the growth of individuals. It has been included here because this growth is the result of autopoietic processes on a subsystem level.

Although it is conceivable that a system or organism could go through changes specific to its life cycle without growth, such instances are rare. Maturation through the life cycle is not synonymous with growth through the life cycle, although the two are often associated. Axiom 6 inherently refers to populations, groups of individuals, or classes of entities, and this is an important distinction from Axiom 5, which refers to the development of single organisms.

In contrast to Axiom V, which is fairly self-contained and in which the transport of raw materials across the system boundary is not made explicit, Axiom 6 specifies processes such as extracting, incorporating, and propagating. Developmental processes (Axiom 5) are circumscribed at a single level, while autopoietic processes imply activity that must be considered at two or more levels.

At this point, let me suggest some conventions to make our language and future discussions clearer. When we discuss individuals in a given system, we address phenomena at Level x. Within the individual, the phenomena are Level $x - 1$ or below. Groups of individuals represent phenomena at Level $x + 1$ or above. Axiom 5 deals with organisms at Level x. Axiom 6, corollary 1, deals with phenomena at Level $x - 1$, and Axiom 6, corollary 2 deals with phenomena at Level $x + 1$.

As we analyze a variety of systems, we may find that at Level $x + 1$ (or greater), phenomena that seemed familiar will suddenly take on new dimensions (see Figure 2-2).[2] For example, growth, understood as a process, takes place along the dimension of time. As physicists explain it, if space is represented in three dimensions, time may be represented as a fourth dimension (see Einstein).

But is the passage of time the same at Level x as it is at Level x + 1? Is not time for the organism, ontogenetic time, a different experience than time for a species, phylogenetic time? If ontogenetic time is fourth dimensional, perhaps phylogenetic time is fifth dimensional. If we, as humans at Level x, understand time as the subjective experience of the fourth dimension, then time for our species may be its experience of the fifth dimension. In the next chapter, we will more fully explore the implications of these concepts.

What does it mean, then, that a system, say at Level x, grows? It means that the components at a level below x increase or multiply. These changes at Level x - 1 will lead to changes at Level x, but should not threaten the integrity of the system at x.

Back to our amoeba example. Before an amoeba divides, changes precede mitosis. The organism itself must mature. It must attain a mass and level of functioning (sometimes called "health") that will allow it to engage in cell division. Next, genetic material divides; the nucleus and other organelles divide as a precursor to the event of cell division. Throughout this process, the amoeba maintains its autonomy.

Another example would be a multicellular organism, a cat for instance. As a kitten, it matures and gains mass at Level x.

---

[2] The designation of a level as x or x + 1 is merely a convention for discussion and is completely relative. There is no absolute Level x, and what is at that level for the purposes of one discussion, may be at x + 1 or x + 2 or x - 1 for other discussions.

Internally, its individual organs grow and develop at Level $x - 1$; connections between tissues form as a function of normal, healthy growth. Individual development at Level x (the developmental principle) entails the activities specified at Level $x - 1$ or below (the first corollary of the autopoietic principle). The processes specified by the developmental principle and the autopoietic principle are different but inseparable. (See Figure 2-2.)

The growth of individual systems, or ontogenetic growth, is best considered in the context of a boundary. In describing the two essential features of living systems, Maturana and Varela (1987) speak first of autopoiesis and secondly of autonomy. *Autonomy* refers to functioning that is independent of other parts. Maturana and Varela's use of the term is consistent with the integral principle of Axiom 2: A system must function independently in some meaningful way for it to be considered autonomous.

Yet autonomy is relative; no boundary is impermeable, and no system functions in isolation. Despite the fact that materials travel across a boundary, ontogenetic growth takes place *within* a boundary and augments autonomy. The boundary is a convention that denotes autonomy.

Population growth is represented in the *second corollary* of Axiom 6. It states: *Population growth is exponential unless limited by an external boundary, lack of resources, or other constraints.*

The simple fact, formalized since Malthus, is that populations grow. This autopoietic process is, to many, the essential characteristic of life. Autopoietic growth that takes place at the subsystem level (corollary 1) is bounded by the system boundary. In fact, providing a barrier to unchecked growth may be one of the more important functions of a system boundary. Growth at the metasystem level, phylogenetic growth (corollary 2), is usually constrained by metasystem boundaries—that is, external factors such as availability of resources.

Let us draw a distinction between the growth of an organism (Axiom 6, corollary 1) and the growth of a population (Axiom 6, corollary 2). If individual growth represents an ontogenetic unfolding in time, does population growth represent another kind of phylogenetic unfolding or development? Ontogenetic growth happens to an individual, while phylogenetic growth is extra-organismic. The former takes place within the perspective of an individual, while the latter is, by definition, beyond any single individual.

The parallel between the propagation of cells within an organism and the propagation of individuals within a population represents the two corollaries and two levels of the autopoietic principle. Following this line of thought, it is possible to think of a population as a kind of superorganism. Such conclusions are consistent with DST as it is being developed here, and lead to interesting possibilities.

In addition, they are consistent with the theory of *punctuated equilibria* (Eldridge & Gould, 1972; Gould, 2002). Briefly, this theory holds that species do not arise gradually, as Darwin's original formulation suggested, but come about abruptly due to historical accidents (the *punctuated* part), and then are maintained for millennia in a relatively stable state (the *equilibria* part) until they die out. Populations, consistent with this view, may be thought of as entities that have a life cycle (Axiom 5) and are capable of self-replication (Axiom 6).

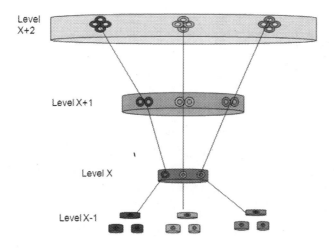

Figure 2-2: Levels of Systems

These ideas are consistent with the notion that a rapid acquisition of genomes may accelerate, even enable, the process of evolution. This is only one of the ways in which this type of systems thinking can contribute to our understanding of the natural world (see Margulis, Sagan, & Mayr, 2002).

Transitioning to the Transformative: Beyond Boundaries

Analytic science, with its emphasis on reduction of wholes into parts, rarely focused on how parts come together to form wholes, or why. Yet this is precisely where systems theory begins, with the whole at some given level of analysis—a cell, a plant, a person. Because of its traditional focus on end states or final forms, systems theory has close links to the philosophy of vitalism and is often susceptible to charges of teleology.

Teleology is a doctrine dating back to Aristotle that seeks to explain nature in terms of purpose, design, or final causes. Teleological explanations, for example, would be that a house exists for people to live in, bees exist to pollinate flowers, animals exist to feed man, and man exists to celebrate the glory of God. What began for Aristotle as a type of causality, became for theists the final cause for the existence of the natural world, i.e., the world exists as it does because God intended it that way.

The vitalists of the eighteenth and nineteenth centuries, while eschewing God in their nature philosophy, nevertheless held a teleological bias that life, separate from the inanimate world, explains itself. The world exists as it does so its creatures can live as they do. Teleological justifications, because of these past philosophical arguments, are suspect and considered anti-analytic and nonscientific.

Von Bertalanffy rejects teleological explanations outright, and sees them as misconceptions of causality and finality in scientific explanation (von Bertalanffy, 1968, pp. 77–80). It is not that systems don't exhibit equilibria phenomena, such as homeostasis in organisms or dynamic equilibria in populations. It's just that the causes of these phenomena are to be understood as deriving from structure, or the nature of open systems themselves, with no recourse to future or final states. Von Bertalanffy holds that open systems are fully understandable from the natural laws of systems theory and teleological notions such as vitalism are "empirically unjustified" (p. 79).

But the idea of final causes is disturbing on another level. Yes, the connections to teleology, vitalism, and theism are unacceptable characteristics for a modern scientific theory. Yes, it defies common sense and physics to think of causes residing in some future time, influencing events in a backward direction. Fruit does not grow on trees so humanity can have food, any more than oxygen exists so animals will have something to breathe. These ideas arose in times when the human being was the measure of all things—when the world, and all that was in it, was, at least in principle, knowable. The idea of final causes implies a changeless universe in which knowable objects exist, caused by a knowable series of events.

Yet evolutionary theory and modernity have combined to teach a very powerful lesson: Certainty, absolute prediction, and all other forms of positivism are illusory. From Heisenberg's uncertainty principle to the importance of randomness in natural selection to chaos theory, we have learned in the last century that nature is not merely difficult to predict, but inherently unpredictable. Periods of stability and structure, the stuff of Newtonian physics, yield unpredictably to quantum leaps and "bifurcations" that in turn produce "order from chaos" (Prigogine & Stengers, 1984). In the language of dynamic systems theory, chaos at one level yields to order at the level above.

The seventh and final axiom of this series recognizes the capacity, even tendency, of complex systems to be inherently unpredictable.

Axiom 7: **The elements of systems have the capacity to reorganize in fundamentally unpredictable ways to create new structures within levels, and new levels.**

This axiom refers to the *synthetic principle* operative in all systems, which allows for potentially new combinations of elements. It accounts for systemic change and evolutionary processes that characterize the capacity of living things to meet new environmental challenges. Autopoiesis (Axiom 6) helps us understand how our world becomes filled with life. Synthesis (Axiom 7) helps us understand the *diversity* of that life.

The fundamental unpredictability of these reorganizations does not mean they are lawless or mystical. They violate none of the accepted principles of analytic science, which are essential to understand the mechanisms of life. In fact, all of the axioms of systems theory are and must remain consistent with analytic science. The agenda of systems theories in general, and DST in particular, is complementary to the agenda of analytic science. The complement of analysis is synthesis. Analytic science teaches us how to break wholes into their constitutive parts; systems science teaches us how those parts come together.

At its most prosaic, within a system level, synthesis (Axiom 7) may be confused with differentiation (Axiom 3). Both address the emergence of new structures, and perhaps the distinction is only a matter of degree. However, synthesis is meant to convey a discontinuity, while differentiation is a more gradual, less revolutionary process. Differentiation is to some degree predictable, while synthesis is inherently unpredictable.

For example, as a business grows, it performs a variety of functions. It differentiates into departments and divisions (Axiom 3). Sometimes businesses come together, as when AT&T acquired NCR. Sometimes they split apart, as when Hewlett-Packard launched Agilent or when Ernst & Young sold its consulting business to Cap Gemini, substantially changing both companies.

These are examples of synthesis (Axiom 7). Synthesis should be understood in its Hegelian sense, as an incorporation of a thesis and antithesis into a wholly new entity that is a synthesis. A true synthesis is transformative. But as the above examples show, synthesis is not always additive. Ernst & Young lost a piece of itself, thereby transforming both Cap Gemini and the organization that Ernst & Young had become. It is that ability to change, to transform, to morph into whole new areas that captures the full intent of the seventh axiom.

It is only with this final axiom that we can now have a full picture, a fully systemic understanding, of the diversity of life on the planet. The synthetic principle in particular allows us to appreciate the branching patterns on the tree of life, the phenomena of speciation. Species arise for a variety of reasons that are both complex and multiply determined (Mayr, 1970). But the seventh axiom, the synthetic principle, allows us to include the fact of different species and the transformation of one type of life into a new type in dynamic systems theory.

Conclusion

The synthetic principle is a fitting capstone to the list of systems axioms, and brings us full circle back to the emergent principle. It is only from the new and unexpected synthesis of elements at one level of a system that new levels arise. The first and seventh axioms are linked. One gives rise to the other. Each creates the conditions for the other. Let us turn to cell biology for an example.

At one time, early in the history of life on this planet, the only living organisms were prokaryotic cells—bacteria-like creatures that are among the simplest possible manifestations of life. The question is, how did eukaryotic cells evolve? Lynn Margulis has suggested a scenario that well illustrates the principles of systems theory: The earliest creatures were not all alike. Even in that primal sea, there was differentiation (Axiom 3), an ecosystem of different prokaryotes adapting and competing for resources.

At some point, two or more of these prokaryotes joined forces and found that they could outhunt and outlive their peers in this way, through a mutual cooperation. The hypothesis, which is now generally accepted, is that the parts of a modern eukaryotic cell were at some primeval time independent organisms. The nucleus, the mitochondria, the ribosomes, and even the flagellum were all at one time separate creatures. They came together to function in a unified, albeit differentiated way (Axiom 3). In so doing, they demonstrated an integrity and coordination (Axiom 2). They shared a common fate and, apparently, met with more success than failure. The nucleus served as a leading part, coordinating much of the new creature's activities (Axiom 4). As new, whole creatures, they lived and died (Axiom 5) and proliferated (Axiom 6). Life on the planet had achieved a new level of complexity (Axiom 1), a different level of organization than had existed before this synthesis (Axiom 7).

Summary: The Axioms of Dynamic Systems Theory

Axiom 1: Emergent Principle

> Nature is organized in levels such that each level comprises a number of elements that, taken together, form an element of the next level.

Axiom 2: Integral Principle

> Any viable system can and must function as an integral whole at some point in its life cycle, despite its ultimate refractability or summativity.

> Corollary 1: Any system can be broken down into component parts (refractability).

> Corollary 2: Any system can be combined with other systems to create additional levels of systemic organization (summativity).

Axiom 3: Differentiation Principle

> Systems tend to become increasingly complex and to differentiate their parts such that each performs different functions in the service of the whole.

Axiom 4: Hierarchical Principle

> The components of complex systems will tend to organize around leading parts, thus producing hierarchical structures in systems.

Axiom 5: Developmental Principle

> Over time, systems change in regular and predictable ways during the course of their life cycle.

Axiom 6: Autopoietic Principle

> Living systems have the ability to self-replicate by extracting raw materials from their environment and incorporating these materials for purposes of system maintenance and propagation.

> Corollary 1: Through transportation-transformation processes, a system is capable of sustaining and augmenting its functions throughout its life cycle.

> Corollary 2: Population growth is exponential unless limited by a boundary, lack of resources, or other constraints.

Axiom 7: Synthetic Principle

> The elements of systems have the capacity to reorganize in fundamentally unpredictable ways to create new structures within levels and new levels.

3

THE PHILOSOPHY AND SCIENCE OF DYNAMIC SYSTEMS

This chapter is a further elaboration of the implications of the seven axioms that comprise dynamic systems theory. While this chapter may seem overly technical to some readers, it establishes the depth and robustness of the theory, and shows that it can respond adequately to initial critiques. It also serves to establish DST as a critical linchpin between science and philosophy, and between the natural and social sciences.

The *Matrioschka* Principle and the Emergence of Levels

For this aspect of systems, one might visualize the little Russian *matrioschka* dolls that nest into each other. Packed, they are a compact collection of figurines that form a solid unit. They also come apart, each doll capable of standing on its own, from tiny to large. Each doll represents a level in our discussion of systems. There is an organic wholeness; the dolls are linked. One comes from the other—emerges out of the other, so to speak. This emergence is a key feature of DST.

Emergentism, the principle featured in the first axiom, is a doctrine that provides "a way of interpreting evolution without having recourse to mechanistic, vitalistic, reductionist, and preformationist ideas" (Goudge, 1967, p. 474). It is a cornerstone of DST. Emergentism seeks to explain evolutionary phenomena by emphasizing the discontinuity of new life forms with old. At the same time, the biosphere is understood as an interconnected succession of levels, distinct from yet related to each other like Chinese boxes or Russian dolls.

Emergentism seeks to be consistent with the data of evolutionary biology, but it is in contrast to the gradualism of Darwin, who felt that new forms arose gradually and were continuous with older ones. The principles of emergentism have been embodied in the theory of punctuated equilibrium, an attempt by evolutionary biologists to explain the life cycle of species (Eldredge, 1985; Eldredge & Gould, 1972; Gould, 2002). Recently, a radical view of emergentism has been suggested by the noted biologist Lynn Margulis and her collaborators (2002) that challenges both gradualism and natural selection. Margulis's ideas are particularly intriguing in light of DST.

Emergentism is a close cousin to epiphenomenalism, although the doctrines are associated with distinctly different areas of science. Emergentism deals with problems in evolutionary biology, while epiphenomenalism is one of several potential solutions to the mind-body problem. The major difference between the two doctrines lies in the type of causality associated with them. *Epiphenomenalism* states that mind and mental activity are the result of brain processes; brain activity gives rise to mind in the same way infection gives rise to fever. Causality goes in one direction and one direction only for the epiphenomenalist, never the reverse. *Mind never impacts brain.*

Emergent properties also result from the activity of a level below, but there is nothing in the doctrine that prevents causality from working bidirectionally. So, for example, to say that life arises as an emergent phenomenon from organic compounds is not to say that living things cannot affect organic compounds. Or if society is emergent from the activity of individuals, social phenomena can nevertheless affect those individuals.

No one, to my knowledge, has connected these two doctrines before, but their parallels seem obvious. In both concepts, one set or class or level of phenomena gives rise to a very different set of phenomena. The relationship between the two levels is obvious yet unclear.

I must confess, however, to an abiding discomfort with epiphenomenalism. It is counterintuitive in the extreme to believe that minds do not affect bodies. Emergentism seems to have no such causal constraints, and therefore seems preferable, both as a solution to the mind-body problem and as a doctrine for understanding the evolution of life.

Emergent properties are a mystery: For some, they are the central mystery, while for others they are useful "if only by giving a name to that which does not respond to reductive analysis" (Medawar & Medawar, 1983, p. 232). Sciences have historically dealt with central mysteries in three ways: by trivializing, analyzing, or axiomizing.

Trivialization involves deciding that some unknown just isn't important enough to waste time on, or that the answer is so obvious it is hardly worth investigating. Needless to say, one generation's trivial question is another's central mystery, but this is a complex issue involving history, zeitgeist, and other cultural idiosyncrasies peculiar to time and place. Trivialization is a conspiracy to ignore an inconsistency in a culture's worldview.

Analysis, by contrast, is a way to focus in on a central mystery. It characterizes the scientific method, which reached its zenith in the twentieth century. Although often a lone genius sparks the analytic process (e.g., Newton, Darwin, Einstein), the method achieves its power by reducing unmanageably large questions into smaller, more circumscribed, but easier to answer ones.

Consider the analogy of ants wandering aimlessly around a forest. One ant, through luck, perseverance, brilliance, or a combination of the three, happens upon a large and tasty morsel. She signals to the others, and they come and together reduce the unmanageable whole into bite-size pieces. Analysis means to break down into parts. This seems to correspond to the image of science propounded by Thomas Kuhn, who differentiated between revolutionary science (the lone exploring ant) and normal science (the legions who follow, to analyze and digest).

The third alternative is to axiomize. An axiom is a proposition or principle that provides a starting point, however artificial, and requires no further proof: for example, the axioms of geometry. This may strike some, especially those partial to analysis, as cheating, but it has several advantages. Axioms provide an agreed-upon point of departure, the givens that a system of knowledge builds upon. The existence of God may be considered an axiom for theological discussion, not perhaps because it is so self-evident but because it provides a basis from which any meaningful discussion about God must proceed. (Proofs of God may be thought of as concessions to the analytic mode and, partly for this reason, are rarely convincing).

Some might argue that analysis, in contrast to axiomization, fails because of infinite regress. That is, there are always smaller particles, more elementary building blocks, to analyze. The current state of modern particle physics demonstrates these problems. Yet it is difficult to shake the feeling, at least for the modern mind, that there is something artificial and arbitrary about axioms, that there must be a level below that is somehow more fundamental. In some sense this is an empirical and practical question. If the goal is to explain, it remains to be seen if the uncovering of additional levels adds to or detracts from explanatory power.

Axioms are a heuristic device that may serve to mediate between the tendencies to trivialize and analyze. They are explanatory way stations that allow for synthesis, model building, prediction, and interpretation without precluding further analysis later as the data warrant. Axioms chart a middle course, describing the world in such a way that it can still be appreciated analytically or mystically. Taken as a gestalt, they begin to map the parameters of a biodynamic worldview.

The Dance of Life: Interorganismic and Environmental Interactions

The seven axioms and their corollaries were discussed at length in Chapter 2, from levels as diverse as the subcellular and the international. While dynamic systems theory enhances our ability to analyze and understand a given system at a given level, the potential of this theory goes far beyond this type of analysis. By attending to the connections between levels, the interactions between systems, and the recognition of patterns of functioning at various levels, we begin to glimpse the rich interconnectedness among living systems that is at the core of DST and its seven axioms.

As stated explicitly in Axiom 1, and implicitly throughout our discussion, systems in nature appear to exist at various levels. These levels are typically characterized in terms of complexity, referring either to numbers of elements or the connections between elements. As discussed in the context of Axiom 1, there is an implied order to the levels that seems self-evident to anyone familiar with the classification of living and nonliving systems. In terms of a systems theory, Boulding (1966) has attempted a classification of levels that, while not necessarily the final word, is certainly useful. He suggests a classification scheme of nine levels, from static structures to transcendental systems.

Boulding's System Levels	
System Level	*Example*
i. static structure	frameworks
ii. simple dynamic system	clockworks
iii. cybernetic system	thermostat
iv. open system	cell
v. genetic-societal system	plant
vi. mobile system	animal
vii. symbolic system	person
viii. social system	family/organization
ix. transcendental system	?

Systems Hierarchy
(Levels of Organization)

Biosphere
Society-Nation
Community
Family
Two-Person
Person
Experience & Behavior
Nervous System
Organs/Organ Systems
Tissues
Cells
Organelles
Molecules
Atoms
Subatomic Particles

(Engel, 1980. pp. 137, 535–544)

There are places where Boulding's classification is somewhat arbitrary, others where it may be incomplete. For example, the difference between level (v), plants, and level (vi), animals, may be nothing more than a certain type of mobility that, while important, does not warrant a completely separate level of classification. Complex plants and complex animals represent different but equally intricate histories of evolution, and our bias in placing mobile animals "above" immobile plants may not be justified. After all, plants in their way are mobile enough to meet their needs.

As an example of incompleteness, at level (viii), social systems, the classification schema seems deficient. Social systems may be divisible into more than one level at this point. Do families, extended families, tribes, villages, organizations, and nation-states really belong to only one level of analysis? Can the level Boulding calls "social" be usefully divided into several levels? This question will be discussed in future chapters. Boulding does deserve credit, however, for the first such systems schema.

Boulding's classification schema provides a structure for Axiom 1—a framework or skeleton, as he refers to it. Alternative frameworks exist but all are relatively equivalent and cover the same ground.

An important principle of systems that these hierarchies allow us to consider is *isomorphism*. Isomorphism (from the Greek *iso,* "same," and *morphic,* "structure") refers to similar structures that may be found at different levels within a system. It is a phenomenon that allows us to compare systems at several levels. Isomorphism may refer to global comparisons between systems, or comparisons between parts of different systems or subsystems.

For example, one might say that a cell is isomorphic to a medieval town. Roughly speaking, they exhibit comparable structures. In terms of boundaries, the cell has a membrane and the city has a wall. The cell transports food in and processes it, while the city uses resources from surrounding farms and forests for the same purpose. Over time, as the cell grows, it may divide or become more complexly differentiated. Likewise, the city can develop suburbs or grow to become larger and more bureaucratic. (Note that growth, given enough time, often results in differentiation and autopoiesis.)

Isomorphism may be evident in more constrained analyses as well. For example, family systems therapists, who treat dysfunctional families by using the principles of systems theory, frequently note repeated patterns of conflict among subsystems. For example, the conflict between a father and son in one generation is repeated in the father-son relationships of subsequent generations.

When similar principles are applied to organizations, a personal conflict between two vice presidents may result in an isomorphic lack of cooperation between the divisions they manage. Or, in another example from the business world, it is not unusual to see an executive falter in a particular job or role, and then to find his or her replacement experiencing almost precisely the same problems—new person, same system dynamics.

Isomorphic patterns exist in these systems because elements are often in constant and similar relationship even when specific system members change. So, in our previous example, two successive manufacturing executives may fail, despite very different personalities and abilities, because a tight labor market, old equipment, and inadequate information technology continue to constrain the performance of one element—in this case, the VP of manufacturing.

Dynamic systems theory makes use of isomorphism in a way that other systems theories do not. In part this is because DST is more focused on the social sciences than the other systems theories.[1] Its axioms are derived not only from theoretical modeling, but

---

[1] Psychoanalytic theory is a curious exception here in that it does overtly deal with social phenomena. I am a great admirer of Freud, having spent a good bit of my professional career studying and writing about his works (Sirkin & Fleming, 1982; Sirkin, 1990, 1992). However, the truth is that many of Freud's ideas have been coopted by the psychiatric and psychological communities that make a living from his work. Discussions of Freud's work often take on mental health dimensions that are not always useful or appropriate in systems discussions. Having said this, I do think that biodynamics augments psychodynamics and vice versa. But this work of integration, although approached superficially in Chapter 5, will have to await future efforts by myself and others.

also from the needs and realities of the family systems and work systems from which it was derived. DST offers the potential, not only for a unified approach to the social sciences, but for a framework to integrate the biological and social sciences. From the behavior of microscopic collectives to national collectives, the axioms and their corollaries are universally applicable.

This is consistent with E. O. Wilson's (1998) consilient agenda, alluded to in the first chapter. Wilson, the leading biologist of his generation, has demonstrated that many of our theories, in different domains, are beginning to converge: genetics with biochemistry, evolutionary theory with comparative biology, and so on. DST and the biodynamic approach seem to address a number of issues, particularly in the realms of psychology, sociology, and economics, that other theoretical approaches ignore.

The Functions of Life: Another Look at Process

Isomorphism provides a tool with which to understand the interconnectedness between organisms and the levels of organismic organization. Isomorphism is essentially a structural principle that interconnects the levels of systems. But structures are inherently static. A *dynamic* systems theory implies an equal emphasis on interaction, process, and function. Note that in Axioms 2, 3, and 5 (the principles of integration, differentiation, and development, respectively) the term "function" is used; add Axiom 4 if "to organize" is considered a function. Clearly, functional processes are integral to DST.

As every noun needs a predicate, so every structure needs a function. Life is not simply about being; it is about doing. As six of the seven axioms attest, we cannot imagine life without its concomitant processes and functions.

Although these two words have been used interchangeably in our discussion of systems, there is an important distinction. *Process*, from the Latin "to go forward", implies a generic activity, some movement over time. *Function*, on the other hand, from the Latin "to perform," conveys purpose, or goal-directed activity toward a specific end. Functions, as a concept, come dangerously close to the teleological fallacy discussed earlier. But as long as functions are not mistaken for final causes, this error can be avoided. Functions serve the system, ensuring survival and continuity. An exhaustive list of abstract system functions has yet to be proposed, to say nothing of universally accepted.

In DST, two functions, development and autopoiesis, have been given axiomatic status. Although these axioms may also be two aspects of a single function, i.e., growth, I will maintain the current distinction as both substantive and practical.

In addition to growth, universal system functions may include defense, metabolism, and communication. There may be more functions in addition to these, or these functions may be broken down into related subprocesses. The goal is not to specify every possible function, but to lay the groundwork. It is perfectly reasonable to expect that at various levels in various types of systems, different functions and functional language will emerge. There are limits to isomorphism. Every system exhibits functions that enable it to interact with other systems at its own and connected levels of organization.

Taken together, these functions, and the concomitant structures upon which they rely, *are* the system.

Energy: The Coin of the Realm

Processes involve energy. They use it, manipulate it, take it in, send it out, store it, and change it. Einstein taught that energy and matter were two sides of the same coin: the entire universe, as it is known, exists on an energy-matter continuum.

The first law of thermodynamics (as amended by Einstein) tells us that all energy-matter processes involve a conservation principle. That is, energy and matter are neither created nor destroyed. The second law of thermodynamics states that any physical process, as a function of using energy, yields an increase in randomness or disorder. According to the second law, entropy, which is equivalent to randomness or disorder, tends to increase over time in the universe as a whole.

As we discussed in the previous chapter, the phenomena of life seem to be at odds with the principle of entropy. It is this gap between the physical and life sciences that DST seeks to fill. Life, in all its various forms, seems to increase the amount of organization in the world; life processes are little islands of negative entropy. They operate in apparent contradiction to, but ultimately are consistent with, all known physical laws.

It is this ultimate consistency with physics that leads us to conclude that the vitalists, the early precursors to systems theorists, were wrong. Life is not a phenomenon separate from the physical world—it is only more complicated. Any viable systems theory must ultimately be consistent with the laws of the physical universe in which those systems reside. This is the ultimate goal of the consilient agenda, as set forth by E. O. Wilson (1998): All the scientific disciplines should inform each other and should be continuous, or at least consistent, with each other.

DST, and the biodynamic approach that it informs, is a workable backdrop, an integument of sorts, which provides numerous connections among different scientific disciplines. The concentration in the following pages will be on the connections among psychology, politics, economics, business, comparative biology, and ecology.

According to information theorists, who greatly influenced early systems theory, information is technically negative entropy. The power of information lies in the implied organization that it communicates. Information may be an intermediate and highly stable state of energy that can be maintained indefinitely. Ultimately this information gets translated into metabolic processes, such as photosynthesis or respiration, which eventually lead to the controlled release of energy in the service of the second law of thermodynamics. Once energy is released, entropy increases. But it is the intermediate steps, the capture and manipulation of raw energy, that are essentially the dance of life. Information is the music that propels the dance.

Systems Science and Its Critics

Let's begin this final section by reviewing the axioms and what they accomplish for dynamic systems theory as a theory. DST seeks to understand and explain wholes—how they come together and work together—as opposed to parts. DST stands in contradistinction to the analytic sciences, which fulfill their program by analysis ad infinitum: the continual breaking down into smaller and smaller parts. To the extent that DST describes a reality in a useful way, it will be a useful tool. These descriptions are understood as rough approximations, models, or maps, never the thing-in-itself, which remains ultimately unknown and unknowable. As Gregory Bateson reminded us, "The map is not the territory, and the thing is not the thing named" (Bateson,

1979, p. 30). Our best theories are only models, maps for partially known and partially unknown territories, and their utility is determined by how well they guide us.

The first axiom stands alone because it describes the entire system of systems that DST addresses. This is the so-called Russian doll view of nature, the view that the universe is a series of interconnected yet distinct worlds within worlds. I used the example of mind as an emergent property of brain cells and brain structures. Minds, of course, become the elements of social systems.

The next three axioms, two through four, are axioms of structure characterized as structural solutions to problems of living. The principles of integration, differentiation, and hierarchy are characteristic of all functional, living systems. A system exists as an integral whole (Axiom 2), even though several systems may work together (summativity) or be broken down into their component parts (refractability). We saw a tendency in systems to differentiate their parts such that the elements become specialized for particular purposes that suited the system (Axiom 3). From this tendency we saw the related phenomenon of "hierarchalization"— that is, the tendency of specialized parts to develop into natural hierarchies around leading parts (Axiom 4). Differentiation and hierarchalization serve essential and ubiquitous functions that ensure survival and continuity—for example, defense, metabolism, and communication.

Axioms five through seven are characterized as axioms of process. Systems tend to develop in regular and predictable ways over time (Axiom 5), and this axiom allows us to consider systems in time. The autopoietic principle (Axiom 6) permits us to consider multiple systems in multiple dimensions over time. Living systems can self-replicate both in terms of their component parts (Axiom

6, corollary 1) and entire populations (corollary 2). The growth specified in this axiom is another essential function of all systems. In discussing this axiom, the concepts of multidimensionality and levels of systems analysis, i.e., Level x, Level $x + 1$, and Level $x - 1$, were introduced. (See Figure 2-2.)

Finally, there is the synthetic principle (Axiom 7). Synthesis is the process by which systems combine their elements to create essentially new systems. Synthesis transforms systems in unpredictable and discontinuous ways. Chaos theory (Gleick, 1988) gives us some insight into the manner by which such processes occur.

Synthesis differs from the summativity of integration in that summativity refers primarily to extant systems that, although growing, remain fundamentally the same. Synthesis refers to novel systems. To draw from the example in the section on synthesis, if a bacterium adds a structure that enhances it—say a second, thicker cell membrane—that is summativity. The system is enhanced, but not essentially changed. But if a bacterium enters a mutual symbiotic relationship with another unicellular organism, as the first eukaryotic cells were thought to have done, that is a true synthesis.

Another aspect of summativity worth noting is that systems may work together without becoming transformed. Dogs hunting together as a pack are a system different from a single dog, but not necessarily a fully reorganized system at Level $x + 1$. Perhaps systems created by summativity are intermediate to systems created by synthesis. Whether these are seen on a continuum or in terms of a discontinuity is less important than differentiating between systems that come together in a casual way and those that are permanent syntheses.

I am willing to concede the possibility that the difference between summativity and synthesis may not be a trivial problem. If everything that works together is a system, then anything is a system, and the whole concept becomes useless. Critics of general systems theory have stated that, among its other problems, GST cannot specify precisely what is meant by a system. The confusion between summativity and synthesis illustrates this problem.

In fact, this problem also haunts us from the beginning in Axiom 1, when the concept of levels is specified in the first place. What is truly a level and what is simply a convention for discourse? Is a group of dogs hunting together a true level of analysis, or is it some arbitrary point between an individual canine and an entire pack (or species, for that matter)? Where do we draw the line between levels? What is a system and what is not?

If we were seeking mathematical rigor, these questions might be enough to stop us here and now. In fact, it may have been von Bertalanffy's aspiration to a mathematically precise systems theory that led to ultimate failure or at least extreme dissatisfaction with such theories. For example, there is Berlinksi's rather devastating criticism:

> But GST involves the impulse to carry the dramas of mathematical construction to a point at which the entities that result are so painfully swollen and senselessly general that without the surreptitious introduction of a series of corset-like contracting definitions nothing of any interest follows deductively. (Berlinski, 1976, p. 10)

Let us skip such aspirations to rigor and the devastating, though not fatal, criticism that they seem to deserve. Let us acknowledge the importance of mathematics at some advanced stage of theory building, at which the historical sciences have not quite arrived. The quest for rigor can lead to *rigor mortis*.

Rather, a dynamic systems theory should embrace the chaos and unpredictability that is essential to life. DST seeks to describe the world in all its rich detail, achieving a deeper understanding of connection and common underlying principles—to explain this richness, not explain it away. We leave perfect prediction to the Popperians.[2] And if DST doesn't provide the predictive control aspired to by some mad scientists of a bygone era, we can only be thankful for progress. All worthwhile science rests firmly on good description, and we should be satisfied to begin there.

---

[2] Sir Karl Popper, a philosopher of science with roots in logical positivism, held that theories could never be proved, only disproved. His goal, like that of the logical positivists he ultimately rejected, was to establish, absolutely and once and for all, "truth." In his case, it was truth based on what was determined to be false. In our century, Popper, and the logical positivists he left, seem somewhat naïve. Absolute certainty is an aspiration for a bygone era. Certainly in the historical sciences (which includes the social sciences), we must be satisfied with narratives that tell interesting, coherent, but far from provable stories. This is the dilemma of legitimacy that has plagued the soft sciences, holding them to standards that are neither appropriate nor achievable.

4

ORGANIZATIONS AS LIVING ORGANISMS

*I*n *this chapter, we return to the fourth kingdom and the organizational world. The perspective that DST and the biodynamic approach provide enables us to see this world in a new context, as part of a natural worldview that is both scientific and continuous with nature. The economic phenomena discussed in this chapter have tended to be viewed in isolation. From this point forward, the natural world and the economic world are to be viewed as continuous.*

The modern organization can be viewed from a number of perspectives, even if we limit ourselves to the social sciences. The macroeconomic perspective, the microeconomic perspective, the sociological, anthropological, and even ethological perspectives—each represents a kind of lens through which to view and potentially understand the complex workings of the organization.

Psychologists alone have a number of lenses through which to understand corporate structure and the interactions of people within them. Rather than jump right into psychological theories, let's begin with some fundamental and obvious truths.

Organizations as Living Organisms

We are programmed by biology and culture to use human capital—in large groups, in small groups, and as individuals in the context of a larger society. I am among a growing number of management consultants and academics who see the organization as a living, complex organism. It has processes and functions like an organism; it has an anatomy of sorts reflected in its organization chart; it has characteristic ways of interacting with the outside world that reflect its markets; and it has evolved systems that help it adapt and thrive in its current environment, which are reflected in its branding and market positioning.

This is the functional anatomy of a company or business. (See Figures 4-1 and 4-2.)

A single company exists in the context of an industry, where it competes with all the other companies in its industry for all different kinds of capital resources, i.e., financial, human, and

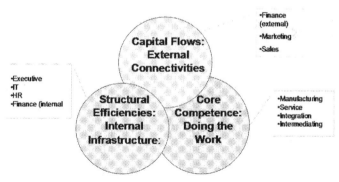

Figure 4-1: Detailed Functional Anatomy of a Business

customer. This is the economic landscape in which business transpires, in which companies are born, grow, merge, divest, falter, and die. It is a competitive landscape in which survival of the fittest has been refined to a science. The coin of the realm is not the raw materials that living organisms metabolize, but financial and human capital, which are just varieties of information that humans have adapted to their purposes. (See Figure 4-3.)

Actually, it would be more correct to say that humans have been adapted to serve the organizations to which they have given birth. For we are speaking of nothing less than a new form of life—not simply a new species, but a whole group of species that we refer to collectively as *business organizations*. We will explore the nature of these creatures at later points in this book. At this point, let's simply allow the possibility that human capital and financial capital interact on a plane that is a step beyond the individual human organism.

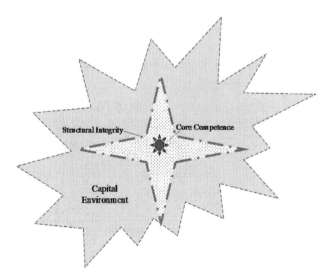

Figure 4-2: The Company as Organisms
in a Capital Environment

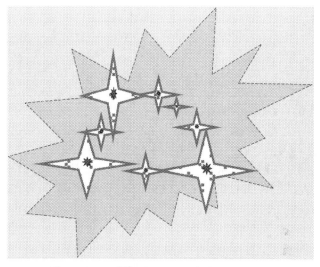

Figure 4-3: The Financial Ecosystem:
Companies in a Capital Environment

The organization as organism is a theme that we will return to again and again. The idea has received quite a bit of attention in recent business literature, and generally is accepted as a truism (see Clippinger, 1999; De Geus, 1997; Rothschild, 1992). However, many writers are only comfortable with this concept as metaphor, whereas I believe it is literally true.

The processes that have created business organisms are the same processes that have driven other forms of evolution on the planet. These processes—evolution and natural selection—represent the most widely accepted and tested scientific theory in human history. Why can't they account for, and to some degree predict, the next phase of evolution on the planet?

The Evolution of Complexity

A few billion years ago, something happened that changed the course of life on earth forever. The primordial sea was filled with simple, single-celled organisms. They were of different shapes and sizes, different adaptive strategies, and different strengths and weaknesses. At some point, an amazing process began to unfold: Some of these organisms began to work together to improve their chances of survival. In a process referred to as *mutualism* by evolutionary biologists, these simple, single-celled creatures began cooperating for their common good. These mutual relationships eventually gave rise to the eukaryotic forms of life: complex, single-celled organisms that contain organelles and other complex structures such as nuclei, mitochondria, chloroplasts, even cilia and flagella (those little hairs or whips that help some cells move along).

These well-known components of cell anatomy are now thought to have been independent creatures at the earliest stages of evolution. The unique abilities of these organelles made them not only useful, but also eventually invaluable to the cells they paired up with, leading to a relationship known as *obligative symbiosis*. The fates of these organisms became inextricably intertwined, and their mutual benefit was so great that they could not live without each other (Margulis et al., 2002).

Fast-forward a couple of billion years. Life has become immeasurably more complex. Organelles within cells, cells within tissues, tissues within organisms, organisms within communities, and communities within ecosystems are all contributing to a vast, biologically diverse tapestry of life on the planet. If there is any pattern to the trends of life and its evolution, it is toward increasing complexity and increasingly complex interrelationships. This is not a straight trend line, but a clear trend nevertheless.

There is a tendency to consider *Homo sapiens*, the most recent branch on the human evolutionary tree, as the most complex of the multicelled organisms. If we order the world according to nervous system development, then humans do win the prize for most complex life on earth. But if we rank life according to social organization, some ant and bee species are the hands-down winners.

In terms of sheer biomass, ants are the most successful organisms on the planet. Their degree of social organization is tremendous, and their ability to colonize vast geographical areas is well known. It is their ability to organize a colony through rigid role structures that has been the key to their success. In a new colony, the firstborn enslave the next born through a combination of biochemical inducements. Roles are established: queen, workers, and others. The workers divide further by size, and their roles change as they grow. The newest workers care for the young. At another stage, they become foragers. The biggest guard the colony. While these strategies, and their complexity, vary somewhat, the pattern remains consistent for most ant species. Bees and social wasps share similar specialization strategies (Wilson, 1971).

What makes a species successful? Again it is a matter of perspective. Early evolutionary theory taught that *survival* was the sole criterion of success. Later the emphasis moved to *adaptation*—it was the ability to exploit a particular environment or environmental feature that made a species successful. According to this view, success is not a single prize or race to be won. Rather it is a never-ending game that each species plays with its environment and the other inhabitants of its ecosystem. The ability to change, in the form of adaptation, becomes a critical component for longevity.

But here again, perspective influences us. Trilobites and dinosaurs were wildly successful creatures by almost any standard—except that they are now extinct. They were well adapted to their environment—except when it changed to a point where it no longer suited them. Humans, on the other hand, arose during an era of wide temperature swings, known as ice ages, and we have been naturally selected for adaptability. Enabled by our large brains, we have developed several capabilities that have permitted us not only to survive, but to grow, adapt, and thrive in ways beyond any other organism or species. All of these capabilities can be expressed or captured in a single word: culture.

Culture is a shorthand way of referring to the social organization in which all humans participate. Language, toolmaking, and role specialization are components of human cultures everywhere. In addition, the simple fact is that humans do live in groups, whether in multigenerational family units isolated from each other or in vast cities.

Essential to the success of human societies, as it is for our distant cousins the social insects, is the ability to develop and live according to specific social roles. In fact, the total number of roles a given society sustains and the average number of roles each adult individual takes on may well be a measure of the complexity of a given society. Culture among humans is perhaps the single development most responsible for our accomplishments. Culture provides a medium in which ideas can be developed, innovations introduced, and the gains of each generation consolidated and built upon.

Cultures are an emergent property of human societies. Organizations are cultures of commerce. They are social groups that have come together for a purpose: to engage in activities that result in the generation of economic capital. Information, in the form of intellectual capital, is both created and utilized in the process.

Emergence of the Fourth Kingdom

Life, as it has evolved on earth, can be characterized as an exquisitely choreographed, amazingly complex handoff of resources that enables the machinery of life to continue. The transfer of energy, in the form of sugars, proteins, and other *biopackets*, is the raison d'être of the food chains that connect species in an ecosystem. Energy, seeded by sunlight, works its way up the food chain, from the simplest to the most complex creatures. All living creatures seem to participate in this grand dance of energy transfer, usually both as consumers of biopackets from species below them to producers of food for species above them. Of course, these relationships are rarely direct and often involve high levels of complexity and interconnectivity among a wide variety of species in an ecosystem.

While the eat-or-be-eaten imperative is certainly a fundamental issue of survival, another issue of equal importance has loomed large in the past century of scientific discovery. If creating and consuming energy is the *what*, then the *how* is found in the molecular genetics of life, in the DNA. The information that resides in every cell is as necessary for its functioning as the nutrients that keep it alive.

So we can say that two parallel processes exist in all life: the ability to use energy, a metabolic process; and the ability to create structure, a genetic process. These two processes are mutually dependent and mutually beneficial—we could not imagine life on earth without them both. The first ensures continuity for the organism throughout its individual life cycle, while the second ensures continuity for the species and its evolution.

But we have moved far afield of the corporate environment. Let's try to wend our way back. While there are several taxonomic classifications available, let's use what I find to be the simplest based on key structural and metabolic elements. Biologists divide life on earth into broad categories known as *kingdoms*. There are three distinctive kingdoms of life on the planet: animals, plants, and protozoa (single-celled creatures). This is the accepted scientific wisdom of our day (see Endnote 1 in Chapter 1 for a fuller discussion).

I want to suggest, however, that right under our noses, a new form of life, a brand-new kingdom, has arisen practically unnoticed.

The kingdom of social organisms could arguably contain the social insects, although our current system of classification has them ensconced among the phylum Arthropoda, which contains insects, spiders, crustaceans, and other hard-bodied creatures. For simplicity's sake, however, let's just look at those social organisms composed of human beings. A social organism, according to this view, is a group of people who come together and function as a dynamic system. This dynamic system both creates and uses social information that permits the social organism to interact with other social organisms.

As discussed earlier in this book, the fourth kingdom has four phyla. They are religions, countries, universities, and businesses. These organizations have structures and core competencies (see Figure 4-1). The competitive landscapes in which they exist— their industries, so to speak—are part of a larger information environment that we call *culture*. Cultures are the seas in which social organisms swim.

In other words, countries exist within a political culture. Corporations exist within an economic culture. Religions coexist in this landscape but according to their own specific cultures, as do universities. And all the denizens of the fourth kingdom interact with each other—businesses with countries with religions with universities.

Human beings in advanced cultures participate in the life of social organisms. They are the interchangeable components of these organisms, in a manner comparable to the way cells constitute animals and plants. Social organisms, at least structurally, exist independently of the humans who inhabit them. Of course they require people to exist, but rarely require any specific person in order to exist. It is common in modern societies for one person to participate in the life of more than one social organism at a time, usually across species. So we can speak of a French Catholic who attends the Sorbonne, or an American Jew who works for IBM.

Roles are the means by which people participate in and contribute to the lives of social organisms. A role is a function evolved by a social organism to enable it to exist and thrive. In the type of social organism we call a country, for example, the head of state, ministers, advisers, elder statesmen, nobles, and senators are roles that countries have evolved to help them survive and exploit resources. History teaches us that this ancient form of social organism, the country or city-state, has grown more complex, but all in all has changed little in 5,000 years.

Evolutionary Economics

A quick history of the evolution of this kingdom, and the phyla within it, will help us better understand the pulls and underlying currents that exist in modern organizations. I present below a timeline of the emergence of key organizational features. Although highly speculative, this timeline does not contradict any known facts and should be regarded as a theory or set of hypotheses subject to further proof and refinement. (See Table 4-1.)

Social apes

Approximately one hundred thousand years ago, but perhaps as recently as fifty thousand years ago, humans eked out an existence as hunter-gatherers. Like the apes from which we evolved, we existed in family-based social units that had explicit, if somewhat complex and fluid, hierarchies. Biological drives and simple emotional states governed much of the behavior of these clans. The search for food dominated social life. These groups were proto-organizational.

Farmers and priests

Approximately ten thousand years ago, an agrarian revolution gave rise to cultivation cultures. Hunter-gathers were forced by their food acquisition strategies to keep moving as they harvested the existing game and wild crops in a given area. Clan size remained small because resources were limited. By contrast, cultivation cultures demanded that people remain in one place year after year. Cultivation enabled and rewarded larger social groupings. Larger, stationary tribes evolved first, but eventually the first city-states emerged in this epoch.

The success of the agrarian strategy led to a crucial social innovation—the emergence of specialized roles in these early societies. No longer was every able-bodied person required to obtain food. Kingly and priestly classes could emerge that contributed to social life by establishing security and continuity (Diamond, 1997). The emergence of belief systems as tools of social control and organization was another feature of this epoch. Both religions and countries evolved during this time as the first denizens of the fourth kingdom. These early cultures were dominated by a search for security in a sense comparable to the hunter-gatherers' search for food. Notice also that these cultures are slowly climbing Maslow's hierarchy of needs, from biological drives to the need for security.

Medieval merchants

About a thousand years ago, at least in Europe, the crumbling ruins of the Roman Empire gave rise to a new economic order that included castle economies and princely states. Global trade routes and the earliest beginnings of modern government arose simultaneously to complement each other as parallel systems of wealth accumulation. This epoch witnessed the beginnings of the third phylum of the fourth kingdom: universities.

Complex government and the accumulation of wealth enabled this epoch to engage in multigenerational projects, such as the building of cathedrals and the exploration and settlement of new territories. Human groups could also engage in wars lasting several generations. The search for and accumulation of wealth characterized this epoch. The earliest business organizations— social systems created solely for the accumulation of financial capital—emerged.

Bankers and moguls

Approximately one hundred years ago, the world saw the proliferation of a new social organism, the fourth phylum of the fourth kingdom, the modern corporation. It should be noted, as in all the previous cases and as in evolutionary biology itself, earlier forms can be found well before this, e.g., the Hudson Bay Company and East India Company. It was only about a hundred and fifty years ago, however, that corporations were granted full legal status on a parity with other organizations. At this point, the emergence of global, multinational economies was in full swing.

Modern societies, by their legal recognition of corporations in the United States and Britain or anonymous organizations in Europe, allowed social groups to act and be treated under the law as "people." That is, a corporation had certain rights as a collective that were formerly granted only to individuals. This allowed for an accelerated concentration of economic capital, the likes of which the world had never seen.

The creation of capital markets, investment vehicles, organized borrowing and credit, and other complex financial transactions has transformed every society. In addition, as corporations grow more complex, countries, religions, and universities grow similarly complex in order to interact more effectively. Biologists refer to this as *coevolution*, and we are seeing it in the fourth kingdom just as we do in other living ecosystems.

Techs, geeks, and infopreneurs

Within the past ten years, we have witnessed the emergence of a new era: the wired economy, also referred to as the digital economy (Tapscott, 1996). The wired economy is both a result and facilitator of the information age. In the information age, knowledge itself, and not simply the tangible result of it as in previous ages, is a valuable commodity. It is an exciting age, and we are seeing a proliferation of corporate forms, from the one-person multinational to the trillion-dollar behemoth.

This is another example of coevolution. As the economy becomes more complex, new forms emerge to take advantage of it. We have seen this before in evolutionary history, which is punctuated by a series of extinctions followed by explosions of evolutionary activity. The most well-known of these is the Cambrian explosion, which saw the proliferation of many animal forms about a billion years ago. Similarly, following the great Permian extinction, we saw an explosion of reptilian species that led to the age of dinosaurs.

In many respects, this age is too new for us to fully appreciate its implications. As our ability to use and create information is enabled by technological innovation, the landscape continues to evolve at an extremely rapid, even unprecedented, pace. The pace of change is changing, and we can't yet tell if this is a permanent feature or something cyclical.

The thrust of these changes seems to be toward mastery: mastery of the environment, mastery of the self, and mastery of the biological and physical world. Technology enables individuals to take control of the production of their own human capital and the human capital of others, which they use in their work. The result is an information upsurge that is giving rise to an explosion of corporate forms, businesses, and industries.

Table 4-1
A Brief History of the Fourth Kingdom

Name	Emerged Approx.	Economic Basis	Chief Characteristics	Nature of Work Activity	Prime Motivation*
Social Apes	100,000	Hunting economies	Tribal/clan organizations	Work leads to food	Search for food
Farmers & Priests	10,000	Agrarian economies	Cultivation cultures	Work entails role specialization	Search for security
Medieval Merchants	1,000	Castle economies	Princely states	Work roles & social roles contribute to a complex economy	Search for wealth (i.e., land, valuable goods, precious metals)

Bankers & Moguls	100	Multinational economies	Corporate actors	Work leads to the accumulation of capital	Search for financial capital
Techs, Geeks & Infopreneurs	10	Wired economies	Networks of networks	Accumulation and management of information	Search for information (i.e., customer needs, science, technology)
* The prime motivation of each level assumes the achievement of goals from the level above, as in Maslow's theory of needs.					

5

ON CONSULTING TO SELVES, GROUPS, AND CORPORATE COMMUNITIES

In this chapter, I pay homage to the psychologists and social scientists who have made significant contributions to my thinking and show the continuities between their ideas and mine. Ultimately, these ideas have a practical and applied value that I demonstrate in this and the following chapters. This chapter has three parts: an introduction to DST, which includes a recap of the history of systems theory; a tour through the theoretical jungle of modern Freudian personality theories, with special emphasis on Harry Stack Sullivan; and finally an effort to connect all this theory to the needs of organizations and organizational consultants. Although ambitious, this chapter attempts to show how DST can help us better understand individuals and organizations by seeing both as complex systems.

Of Bees and Men: The Emergent Nature of Living Systems

Consider the honeybee. Her body possesses the classic insect anatomy of head, thorax, and abdomen. She has wings, compound eyes, and antennae. Her distinguishing features include a stinger with which to defend herself and leg hairs and sacs with which to collect pollen. A perfectly adequate description of a common insect, right?

Well, only up to a point.

The honeybee interacts with other honeybees. She uses an elaborate communication "dance" to inform the others about sources of food. She cooperates with the others of similar and different caste to collect and process food, protect the group, raise young, and procreate. But even this second-level discussion misses an essential and vital point for understanding the honeybee.

The honeybee is a hive creature, a member of a community, which in itself is a superorganism with its own infrastructure, precise divisions of labor, and logic for perpetuating and reproducing itself—a logic that subordinates the good of the individual honeybee to the good of the whole.

There is yet another perspective on the honeybee. The hive itself does not exist in isolation but in an ecological context that includes hive-environment interactions. For example, modern bees and modern flowers have coevolved; neither existed nor could exist in its present form without the other. Bees of the hive have a definite impact on their environment and vice versa. This level too must enter into any full discussion and understanding of the honeybee.

The psychoanalytically oriented organizational consultant is like a biologist trained in insect anatomy who encounters a beehive for the first time. How to make sense of it, how to study it, how to help it function better in relation to its environment—all become important questions, the answers for which the consultant may be at a loss.

Perhaps most important, there is nothing inherent in the bee as an individual insect that would lead our hypothetical insect biologist to predict the hive, or the hive's interaction with its environment. The hive is an emergent quality of bees in the same sense that economic organizations are an emergent quality of humans. The corporation is not reducible to the individual any more than the hive is understood by studying bees in isolation. An understanding of the individual is necessary but not sufficient to understand the organization. This is the phenomenon of emergence.

The Nested Universe and Dynamic Systems Theory

Emergentism is a doctrine that provides "a way of interpreting evolution without having recourse to mechanistic, vitalistic, reductionist, and preformationist ideas" (Goudge, 1967, p. 474). Emergentism seeks to explain living phenomena, including mental life, as *dis*continuous evolution.

At the same time, the living world is understood as an interconnected succession of levels, distinct from yet related to each other, like Chinese boxes or Russian dolls. One level emerges from another, but once it does, it operates independently from the preceding level.

Emergentism seeks to be consistent with the data of evolutionary biology, yet is in contrast to the gradualism of Darwin, who felt that new forms arose gradually and were continuous with older ones. The principles of emergentism have been embodied recently in the theories of punctuated equilibrium and symbiogenesis. *Punctuated equilibrium* is an attempt by evolutionary biologists to explain the life cycle of species and the fact that the fossil record does not support the gradual version of evolution (Eldredge, 1985; Eldredge & Gould, 1972). *Symbiogenesis* is the idea that new species emerge when two or more species come together in symbiotic and permanent relationship, as in the case of lichen (Margulis et al., 2002).

The many levels are interconnected, and it is not possible to fully comprehend any element without taking into account the levels above and below it. For example, in human systems, organelles constitute cells, cells constitute tissues, tissues constitute organs, organs constitute organisms, organisms constitute families, families constitute tribes, tribes constitute societies, and societies constitute nations. The language changes slightly depending on which specific aspects of the human system are under discussion, but the principle remains the same. The fact of the interconnectedness of levels and the manner in which they are nested is a cornerstone of the present attempt to link the psychoanalytic theory of the individual with organizational phenomena. (See Figures 2-1 and 2-2.)

Emergence is the first principle in dynamic systems theory (Sirkin, 1992b, 1994c). DST's goal is to provide conceptual and practical links to areas of clinical work that exist semiautonomously but are connected in important ways. These semiautonomous areas include individual psychotherapy, group psychotherapy, and organizational consultation. DST seeks to create a framework, albeit loose and imperfect, that can encompass these multiple perspectives.

The Individual Mind in Context: Freud, Sullivan, and the Interpersonal Orientation

Each level implicit in the concept of emergence must be understood on its own terms. Each level has a language in which its key concepts are expressed, a nexus of problems with which it is centrally engaged, and a praxis by which it affects the world. Sigmund Koch (1976) has referred to these as *language communities.*

Different language communities must exist between levels, although several language communities may coexist within levels.

At the level of mind, psychoanalytic theory has evolved the most complex language community and one that has dominated ideology and praxis for almost a century.[1] Yet within the psychoanalytic camp, a number of schools or dialects exist and continue to appear year after year (see Munroe, 1955). All speak a psychoanalytic language and are engaged in the practice of psychotherapy, yet with different emphases and somewhat different goals.

Greenberg and Mitchell (1983) have attempted to bring some order to this tower of psychobabble by pointing to a deep divergence in psychoanalytic theory, and by grouping theoretical approaches accordingly. This divergence is between drive/structure models, typified by Freud's original work, and relational/structure models, typified by Sullivan's contributions.

The Classical Drive Model and Reductionism

According to Greenberg and Mitchell (1983):

> The basic unit in classical theory is the individual psyche, and Freud's rich and incisive theorizing is framed by that focus ... Drive/structure model theories are necessarily intrapsychic—the drives

---

[1] Of course, other schools of psychiatry and psychology exist, but none has developed such an integrated body of theory and practice, except perhaps cognitive-behaviorism in psychology and the medical model in psychiatry. Considerations of focus and space prevent these models from being fully considered in the present context.

> by definition originate within the individual mind; the obvious focus of inquiry into drive-derived processes is within the fantasies, wishes, and impulses of the individual. (pp. 100–102)

Even in his work most directly concerned with groups and organizations, Freud restates his individualistic and reductionist bias: "Group psychology is therefore concerned with the individual man," and the so-called "social instinct" may in fact be reducible to more primitive drives (Freud, 1921/1959, p. 2).

Freud's reductionism infuses all of his theoretical writings (Sirkin & Fleming, 1982). The drives are essentially the prime movers of the mental mechanism; they provide a constant influx of energy into the psychic engine. These drives must be harnessed, managed, and controlled, which is the function of many familiar psychic structures and processes (i.e., the ego, defense mechanisms, neurotic symptoms).

Many critics of Freud's drive theory seem to confuse his reductionist program, and a type of psychoanalysis that results from it, with the drives themselves (see Greenberg & Mitchell, 1983). Reductionism, I would agree, is a misguided approach to mind and its social manifestations. At its worst, it is a type of scientism that contributes nothing except a false sense of having arrived at or aimed toward a first cause. Drives, on the other hand, may be indispensable to a coherent model of mind. Before discussing the necessity of drives, however, let us turn next to an alternative to psychological reductionism.

The Interpersonal Relational Model and Contextualism

The opposite of reductionism is *holism*, and general systems theory represents one of the more coherent embodiments of holistic principles (von Bertalanffy, 1968). Whereas reductionist models attempt to reduce phenomena to smaller and more basic parts, holistic models attempt to build from simple elements to more complex systems.

The two approaches may not be mutually exclusive; perhaps they are complementary, like a telescope that can magnify a constricted field when used from one end or permit more inclusion but less detail when used from the other. We cannot, however, look through both ends simultaneously.

Relational/structure models in psychoanalysis are inherently holistic. They tend not to reduce to elements, but rather add elements into more inclusive wholes. Harry Stack Sullivan was an exemplary theorist of this model:

> The basic units in Sullivan's interpersonal theory are the interpersonal field and the relational configurations that derive from it. The individual psyche, in this view, is a part and reflection of a larger whole, and is inconceivable outside of a social matrix ... In Sullivan's system, the self is organized around relational configurations ... structured into the self, which is composed of a collection of prominent "me-you" patterns loosely held together by a set of rationalizations and illusions. (Greenberg & Mitchell, 1983, pp. 101–103)

The interpersonal theory, while not as neatly consistent and elegant as Freud's theory, nevertheless provides a unique view of the human mind based essentially on context and contextual considerations.

Historical Antecedents of Interpersonal Theory

Four great thinkers of the early twentieth century stood solidly beneath Sullivan, supporting his observations and ordering his thoughts: Freud, Meyer, Mead, and Malinowski.

Freud's influence was so pervasive that Sullivan makes little attempt to separate it out: "Needless to say behind all … are the discoveries of Sigmund Freud" (Sullivan, 1953, p. 16). Clearly, though, Sullivan did not swallow Freud whole. He chose carefully which elements of classical psychoanalytic theory to include and which to eschew or reject outright. Many concepts, however, were subtly transformed. For example, while Sullivan seemed to reject the notion of instincts altogether, he made the concept of dynamism a cornerstone of the theory. He defines dynamism as "the relatively enduring pattern of energy transformations which recurrently characterize the organism in its duration as a living organism" (Sullivan, 1953, p. 103).

There are some interesting parallels between Sullivan's dynamisms and Freud's Q, a quotient of energy Freud postulated in 1895 that was the forerunner of his concept of instincts (Sirkin & Fleming, 1982, p. 232). The goal here for both thinkers seems to have been to give the laws of physics their due and acknowledge that all systems, even organic systems, need energy to run. Mental activity was in some way a transformation of this energy. It seems that Sullivan was not strictly antireductionist, simply more preoccupied with the way parts come together than how they look broken down. He seems at least grounded enough in nineteenth-century science to sympathize and try to remain consistent with Freud, the reductionist scientist.

Adolf Meyer, the father of the psychobiological approach in psychiatry, was among the most powerful and influential psychiatrists of his day. The specifics of his theory need not concern us here, since they barely outlasted him. But the influence of his approach had a deep effect on Sullivan and other psychiatrists (Redlich & Freedman, 1966).

Psychobiology viewed man as the apotheosis of an evolutionary chain. While somewhat anthropocentric by today's standards, it nevertheless stressed the connection between the biological level and the human level. Man is first and foremost an animal— an animal with the mental apparatus to experience himself as both subject and object, which is perhaps his most distinguishing feature. More modern perspectives in psychiatry, e.g., the biopsychosocial approach (Engel, 1980), are clearly derived from Meyer, but also acknowledge affinity to a growing body of general systems approaches.

George Herbert Mead was not only among the great philosophers of his day; his influence on American ideas of the self can still be felt (Sirkin, 1990c). Mead was the first to articulate that the self was nothing. The self is a process, an act of being that involves the reflection of appraisals from others and the living out of roles one learns from interpersonal surroundings. The self, according to Mead, is fluid, flickering, continuously self-created, and essentially interpersonal. Sullivan seems to have appreciated the significance of not reifying the self as conveyed in his concepts of "self-system" and "dynamisms."

Malinowski, through the study of cultural anthropology, enabled Sullivan to move from the individual to the interpersonal field, and to the wider arena of society. The activities and thoughts of people are only fully comprehensible in the context of social life: customs, rules, expectations, language, environmental interactions, and common needs and concerns (Sullivan, 1953,

p. 18). Again, Sullivan's continued emphasis on **context** found a natural ally in Malinowski's approach to the study of culture.

The Essence of Interpersonalism

As we trace the influence of these men and their ideas on Sullivan, we begin to see the essential outlines of interpersonal theory. Context becomes all-important, whether biological or social. Full understanding of the self requires a full appreciation of both biological and social effects. Even while acknowledging the profound influence of biology and culture, this conceptualization does not view the self as a passive receptacle of these influences, but as processor, transformer, and transmuter of them as it creates personality from the rhythm and melody of its biological and interpersonal world. Sullivan is anything but a reductionist as he seeks to understand and appreciate this complex dance between self and environment.

This implicit rejection of reductionism qualifies Sullivan as a proto-systems theorist. In this respect he stands in contradistinction to Freud and most of Freud's followers, who implicitly accepted a reductionist paradigm for science and psychology. By stressing the interactive nature of psychotherapy and the interpersonal and dynamic nature of self, Sullivan recognized the futility of the reductionist paradigm. The interpersonal therapist strives not to reduce down but to expand out:

> By widening the patient's awareness of his life, what Sullivan called an 'expansion of the self' is arrived at. One then trusts that the patient can change his own life according to his own canons. Indeed, the therapist carefully avoids acting in a way he hopes will 'cure' the patient. He is interested only in widening the circles of

participant-observation for the patient, until a
sufficient enrichment of his awareness of his life
permits him to change. (Levenson, 1991, p. 164)

Both psychoanalytic-drive theories and interpersonal-relational theories are inadequate if they portray the self as passive or wholly derivative. The self is neither "just" a manifestation or receptacle of drives, nor is it "simply" a repository of interpersonal experience. *The self is not passive.* Gordon Allport, a contemporary of Sullivan, stressed that the self is constantly "becoming" (Allport, 1955), or to use another of his phrases, that it is a *unitas multiplex* (Allport, 1961). To the extent that this "unity in multiplicity" requires effort, even energy, the self may be the result of dynamic forces within the person. These dynamic forces may just as well be termed "drives," à la the Freudians, or "dynamisms," à la Sullivan.

The problem with drive models is the implicit reductionism in the theory, not the drives per se, which are neither atavistic theoretical tendencies (Levenson, 1991, pp. 136–137) nor "the last smoke of evaporating reality" (Mitchell, 1979), as some have held. The self-system, as any system, requires structures and processes that make it functional. These structures and processes allow it to perform functions necessary to its existence, survival, and growth. They permit the system to interact with other systems and the environment, to function collectively and singularly, to develop and change in ways that are universally ordered. These activities of the system are by definition dynamic—that is, they involve forces and they are not static.

These forces are not mystical forces, nor are they metapsychological (in the sense of "beyond psychology", a term Freud often used). They are the plain forces inherent in the physical properties of matter and energy. I suggest that all systems, whether they are self-systems or organizational systems, are dynamic—they are active and interactive and share common features of structure and process, regardless of level. Thus my term *dynamic systems theory*.[2]

These issues lie at the heart of mind-body problem, which has plagued philosophers for hundreds of years. By now it will not surprise the reader that I believe mind is emergent from body, and the mind-body problem is more a question of agreeing on level of analysis and language than of metaphysics.

It is the interaction with other systems, with other minds, that is the essential feature of interpersonalism. This interaction leads us naturally to consider metapersonal systems: groups, organizations, and other human social systems. The interpersonal theory is incomplete without a complementary theory of social organization.

Psychoanalysis is primarily a theory pertaining to intrapsychic development and therapy. Early in Freud's work, he realized the necessity of including significant others, primarily the mother, in his theories. The mother-infant dyad became the cornerstone of most subsequent work involving object relations and interpersonal methods. Psychoanalysis, with the exception of Freud's incomplete forays into group psychology (Freud, 1921/1959) or his brief discussions of the primal horde (Freud, 1913/1950), primarily concerns individuals or, at most, dyads. The discussion in the following sections takes us well beyond Freud's dyads and into the realm of the social.

---

[2] The historian Henri Ellenberger (1970) has traced a multitude of meanings of the term "dynamic" in psychiatry. Although none of these usages contradicts the sense I want to convey, perhaps it is the usage of Hughlings Jackson that comes closest to Freud's notion of mental dynamisms (Sirkin & Fleming, 1982, p. 239) and the concept of "dynamism" that Sullivan also means to convey (Sullivan, 1953, p. 102–103).

Multiple Minds and Metapersonal Systems: New Levels Require New Levels of Discourse

General systems theory

Systems theory is among the most direct attempts to arrive at a coherent body of thought not focused on individuals. A thorough discussion of its origins would take us back at least to the German romanticists and nature philosophers, well beyond the scope of this chapter. The following discussion will not stray beyond the twentieth century.

Ludwig von Bertalanffy (1968), biologist and polymath, suggested the most ambitious statement of a general systems theory. He defines systems as "sets of elements standing in interrelation" and goes on to adumbrate their mathematical and qualitative characteristics (von Bertalanffy, 1968, p. 38ff). One of the core concepts von Bertalanffy introduced is *isomorphism*, the idea that different systems have similar structures and parallel processes. It is the interrelations—not the nature of the elements themselves— that are quintessential in von Bertalanffy's theory.

Although his writing is filled with the mathematical equations one often associates with scientific specificity, it is the very generality of von Bertalanffy's version of systems theory that makes it problematic (Phillips, 1976). Because he deals in so many generalities, von Bertalanffy fails to successfully apply his systems theory to any one body of data or phenomenon. The truth is that general systems theory has fallen somewhat short on its promises.

Bion and the Tavistock tradition of group relations

Wilfred Bion's (1959) *Experiences in Groups* represents a significant departure from any previous psychoanalytic contribution, and is a unique approach to the understanding of groups. Although beginning from a conventional psychoanalytic background, which included an analysis with Melanie Klein, Bion moved beyond conventional theory, even Kleinian theory, by observing that groups functioned as coordinated and intentional wholes. Among his most valuable observations were that groups were capable of functioning at two levels. *The work group level* corresponded to the conscious goals of the group and its members, while *the basic assumption level* corresponded to the unconscious and defensive goals of the group.

Bion identified three types of basic assumption patterns of group attitudes and behavior: dependency, fight-flight, and pairing. Without defining all of these terms in detail, it is sufficient to note that while Bion did not lose sight of the individual, he nevertheless interpreted activities within the group as a manifestation of group goals. His observations and interventions took place at a level above individual psychodynamics, often referred to as the level of "group-as-a-whole."

Bion was fortunate to work with colleagues at the Tavistock Institute in London who were interested in applying and expanding his ideas to a variety of *in vivo* groups and group experiences (Trist & Murray, 1990). In particular, Ken Rice and Eric Miller (Rice, 1963, 1965; Miller & Rice, 1967), along with their colleagues, have discussed the application of these ideas to work groups and organizations. Especially noteworthy is their attempt to integrate Bion's psychoanalytic perspective and Lewin's social field theory (1951) with a general systems theory approach:

> Within this model, psychopathology may be conceptualized as a breakdown of the control function, a failure to carry out the primary task, and a threat to the survival of the system.

In the individual we see breakdown of the ego and emotional regression; in the group, breakdown of leadership and paralysis in basic assumptions; and in the institution, breakdown of the administration, failure to carry out the institutional tasks, and loss of morale. Breakdown of boundary control is the principal manifestation of breakdown in the control function. (Kernberg, 1984/1985, p. 403)[3]

By focusing on the parallel processes, or isomorphism, between levels, and the function of boundary as a maintainer of system integrity, this attempt to blend general systems theory and Bionian psychodynamics comes closest to the goals of DST.

While efforts to integrate general systems approaches with psychoanalytic approaches are laudable, there are limitations due

---

[3] With his social field theory, Kurt Lewin (1951) hoped to do for psychology what Einstein had done for physics. His goal was to establish a basic framework from which to understand human behavior. Originally, Lewin was a member of the Gestalt school of psychology, which emphasized the synthetic functions of mind. His psychological field theory used Gestalt principles, which deal primarily with perception but stress social relations and interactions, i.e., the social field. Lewin's famous formula is B = f (P, E), or behavior is a function of person and environment. This formula is the cornerstone of his social psychology. Lewin believed that one's perception of the social environment, with its incipient rewards and punishments, determined behavior. The social field was the primary determinant of personality and behavior. Lewin's theories and research had wide-ranging effects, especially following his immigration to the United States and his establishment of group research laboratories at MIT. His students went on to found the National Training Laboratories, which spawned the T-group and encounter group movements. Although later adapted for psychotherapeutic ends (Leiberman, Yalom, & Miles, 1973), these groups were originally research oriented, following Lewin's dictum: "No research without action, no action without research." Lewin's tradition of action research can also be found, alive and well, among organizational consultants (Argyris & Schon, 1978).

to significant incommensurabilities among theories. General systems theory, in its current forms, simply claims too much in terms of specific applications from rather general quasi-mathematical formulae (see David Berlinski's (1976) scathing attack on the mathematical assumptions of systems theory). In its desire to be all things to all disciplines, general systems theory has failed to respect the differences between language communities among very disparate disciplines.

The application of Kleinian and Bionian theories to larger systems involves other problems. At the root of Klein's object relations theory are the drives of aggression and love, and secondarily, the feelings of anxiety and need for reparation produced by these primary object drives. Klein's work pertains almost exclusively to individual development and the vicissitudes of the individual's attachments to significant objects. Klein's (1946/1975) introduction of the concept of *projective identification*, as one way that internal psychodynamics utilizes and affects others in the social environment, provides a bridge to group phenomena.

Bion's contributions build upon Klein's. Basic assumption dependency, one of Bion's group defenses, bears many similarities to the infant's relation to the good object or leader. Basic assumption fight-flight, another group defense, similarly manifests the aggressive-paranoid relationship to the bad object or leader. Basic assumption pairing, Bion's third group defense, may represent the group's efforts at repairing the compromised object relations caused by the drives. The basic assumptions are a defense against anxiety.

Among Bion's contributions are his development of a language and terminology at the level of the group, which permitted the development of group-as-a-whole techniques. Bion's contributions are limited, however, by his uncritical incorporation of Klein and Freud. The group-as-a-whole, for Bion, is never more than a collection of individuals who collaborate in work and defense. Although Bion's terminology helps us talk about group-level phenomena, his theories provide little insight into the formation and development of small groups and their relation to larger organizations.

Family systems theory

No discussion of theories of group functioning could be complete without acknowledging the important contributions of family systems theory (Hoffman, 1981). Emerging from a tradition that was explicitly not psychoanalytic, family systems therapies make use of principles of communication theory that emphasize human groups as information processing systems. Despite their acknowledgment of the contributions of von Bertalanffy's general systems theory, the family therapists were most deeply influenced by Gregory Bateson, who as an anthropologist was most sensitive to the social construction of reality and the relativity of epistemology (Bateson & Reusch, 1951; Bateson, 1972, 1979).

Like psychoanalysis, family systems therapy today is no longer unified by allegiance to a single theoretician. And also like psychoanalysis, there is a worldwide network of practitioners united as much by common principles of practice as by theoretical considerations. These shared principles include the use of family mapping, or genograms, to portray the interconnected family system (Guerin & Pendagast, 1976), the use of a developmental theory of the family (Carter & McGoldrick, 1989), and the use of a variety of techniques to realign family communications and interactions (Minuchin & Fishman, 1981).

What family systems theory offers is a theoretical starting point at an interpersonal level, assuming that communication implies interpersonal interaction. The implicit reductionism of psychoanalytically derived theories is avoided by starting with interpersonal communications and the social phenomena that arise because of them. Levenson (1972) believes that such a communication paradigm was among Sullivan's original strengths until Sullivan fell back on an energic/drive model.

Critics of family systems theory say that the field's reliance on early systems theorists tends to lead them to treat the family more like a servomechanism than as an organic system comprised of individuals (Pam, 1993). Organizational consultants have also challenged the uncritical appropriation of family therapy techniques and theory into work at the organizational level, pointing out that techniques developed to work with families don't always generalize to larger, more complex, and task-determined work groups (Borwick, 1986).

Consulting to Organizational Systems: The Art of Working Between Levels

By their very nature, all corporate communities contain a multitude of systems. Subsidiaries, divisions, and product groups are examples of subsystems. Each of these subsystems contains working groups, each of which may contain a few to many individuals.

The task of the consultant using a biodynamic approach is to identify the proper level of system intervention (the emergent principle), to delineate the system in question (the integral principle), and to begin to understand how the system is structured in terms of role clarity and authority (differentiation and hierarchicalization). Essential to an initial diagnosis is an appreciation of the system's history (the developmental principle) and its ability to thrive in current organizational and economic environments (the autopoietic principle). The recognition of potential opportunities for a given system to transform, as well as the consultant's ability to facilitate this process, is the most significant challenge to the organizational consultant (the synthetic principle). These tasks are isomorphic with, or at least have parallels to, those of the interpersonal psychoanalyst as indicated by Levenson (1991).

The consultant cannot stay fixated at one level of systems organization. Like the honeybee flying from flower to flower and to hive and back, the informed consultant must be able to shuttle among levels of organization, from team dynamics to corporate politics to individual psychology and back to the team. The knowledge of the dynamics at both the individual and corporate levels must be integrated into the work at the team level. There are no simple or straightforward rules for this integration, only the general guidelines of a dynamic systems theory.

The art of the consultant lies in the ability to work between levels. The microeconomist may have a better grasp on the economic theory of the corporation, and the psychoanalyst may have a better understanding of individual psychodynamics, but the competent consultant should feel at ease in both worlds. The DST consultant is a facilitator who functions within and between levels.

Selves into group members

When consulting is done at the level of the small group or team, the task is to facilitate formation and functioning of the work group. The delineation of role or roles is essential. Interpersonal theory provides a basis for understanding individual functioning— the characterological distortions and security operations of the self-system as it functions in its interpersonal environment. These considerations must be incorporated into group-level constructs that emphasize "role" and "group-as-a-whole" concepts (Agazarian, 1982, 1992).

Groups into organizations

The organization is a system of work groups held together by coordinated goals and a common organizational infrastructure (e.g., human resources, management information systems, finance, board of directors, etc.). At this level, the consultant facilitates boundary-making that reinforces small group identity while allowing for transformation as a result of new information from subsystems and other parts of the larger system. Intergroup theory and the principles of embedded intergroup relations are particularly relevant at this level of intervention (Alderfer, 1977, 1986).

The systems consultant has a unique relationship with the system being consulted. Consultant and system function independently outside of the consultative relationship, yet it is within the relationship that the work of consultation is done. Psychoanalysts have long recognized both the opportunities and risks of such participant observation. True objectivity is necessarily compromised, but additional insights become possible. Krantz and Gilmore (1991) have discussed this phenomenon as it pertains to organizational consultants.

The consultant stands "meta" to the system—that is, somewhat but not entirely on the periphery. This stance provides flexibility and increased opportunity to facilitate change (Wynne, McDaniel, & Weber, 1986). Yet the consultant, either individually or as part of a consulting group, is a system unto him- or herself. The interactions among consulting systems and organizational systems introduces many additional layers of complexity.

Summary: Dynamic Systems from Individuals to Organizations and Beyond

This chapter, like those preceding it, is an attempt to bridge a theoretical chasm between individual psychology as understood via psychoanalytic theory, and organizational theory and economics. The danger inherent in such an ambitious enterprise is that, by trying to explain too much, it may explain nothing well. The need for a biodynamic approach grounded in DST, however, arose because of these theoretical discontinuities. If the connecting framework that DST purports to be falls short, the need for such a framework nevertheless continues to exist.

As I have suggested, general systems theory seems to have failed somewhat in its goal to make over science in a new image. Is DST simply old wine in a new bottle? Although still a type of systems theory, DST is unique in both the clarity of its axioms and the systems principles that it elaborates.

Although the emergent principle may be implicit in some statements of general systems theory, it is not a part of that theory per se. The explicit use of the philosophy of emergentism in DST and the model of the nested universe provide a unique starting point for the theory. The synthetic principle, incorporating the advances of chaos theory (Gleick, 1987) and complexity (Waldrop, 1992), provides for the recursive evolution of systems and their fundamental unpredictability. The first and last axioms of DST incorporate new advances in evolutionary biology and particle physics, respectively, helping to ensure its relevance at all the different levels that the theory attempts to address. The wine in the DST bottle may taste like an old vintage, but it is distinctly different.

It was Harry Stack Sullivan who first resisted the reification of the self, offering instead the term "self-system." I suggest that Sullivan was in fact a proto-systems theorist, because he recognized in the self a constellation of identifications and relational fragments that were best described as a dynamic system. The self-as-system is not only consistent with DST, it is virtually dictated by the theory.

Interpersonal psychoanalysis, as it moves from self-as-system to interpersonal systems, begs for theoretical constructs that can accommodate larger and larger groups of people. Bionian group theory is consistent with this need, but only advances us one level. When we incorporate DST, the many levels—from self to interpersonal to group to organization and beyond—can be adequately accommodated.

The preceding chapters have attempted to lay a persuasive groundwork that DST can accommodate every level of analysis, from individuals to the largest social endeavors. The theory, however, is not a procrustean bed that insists everything fits neatly into place. It is a tool, but only one, by which to understand a huge and fascinatingly complex world of people interacting in complex ways.

The preceding chapters have been our time together in the laboratory. We have explored the science and the theories behind DST. It has been a protracted but hopefully not wasted effort to understand how those who have come before have dealt with these problems. Now it is time to take a field trip—in fact, several field trips. This is where the world gets interesting, where we encounter real life, where we come face-to-face with the inadequacy of theory in the productive and exciting world of business today.

Part II

THE CHALLENGES TO COME: A CONSULTANT'S PERSPECTIVE

6

LEADERSHIP: MYTHS AND MISCONCEPTIONS

There are so many passionately held but erroneous beliefs about business that deconstructing them can rival a course in Greek or Roman mythology. For that's what many of these notions are: myths. None is more persistent than the idea that companies must and should live forever, and that the end of a business somehow means failure.

To adhere to our biological approach, we must acknowledge that companies and corporations—indeed all organizations—have a natural life cycle. After all, there is nothing more organic than a beginning, a middle, and an end. The average life span of a company in the world today is about twenty-five years—roughly twice that in the case of a Fortune 100 company, since their huge volume, mass, and inertia tend to keep them going longer. But, big or small, companies don't last forever—nor should they.

In this chapter, however, the myths that I want to focus on are those that pertain specifically to leadership.

As any nonfiction reader knows, "leadership publishing" has become a cottage industry, spanning the spectrum from textbooks to quick-reading self-help volumes. Exemplars of leadership can run the gamut from the wisdom of Jesus Christ to the people skills of Jack Welch to the Machiavellian machinations of, well, Machiavelli. Embedded in all of this leadership insight is the implication that leadership is an obvious and clearly recognizable trait. It's not.

The Monolithic Myth

The monolithic myth is a belief perpetuated by consultants and the "leadership industry," as well as by the varying assessments used in the executive coaching field that allegedly measure the trait of leadership. The assumption underlying the monolithic myth goes something like this: Leadership is one, single, big thing, and you either have it or you don't.

The problem? It isn't true. Leadership isn't one thing. It's a collection of aptitudes, skills, and areas of specialized knowledge, often coupled with luck and good timing. Yes, being in the right place at the right time can plunge you into leadership. Leadership isn't based on a single characteristic, but on a constellation of characteristics that come together in different ways in the personalities of different leaders.

Moreover, leaders emerge at various times under varying circumstances, and for a variety of highly specific reasons. It is an individual's particular combination of personal qualities that will determine whether, in a given time, place, setting, and circumstance, he or she will become a leader. The ideal leader needs the perfect environment that allows his or her qualities to flourish—the same way, following our biological construct, a given ecological environment gives rise to a particular life form.

Caesar could only cross the Rubicon in a particular time and place to become the leader of the Roman Empire and set the course of history in motion in exactly the way he did. Had he been born 100 years earlier or later, he would almost certainly not be remembered as—or ever even have been—the great leader that he was.

Similarly, Abraham Lincoln, considered by many historians to be the greatest American leader, came along at a time and in a place that allowed his leadership qualities to make themselves evident. During much of his lifetime, Lincoln's leadership qualities were not particularly obvious, even to those who knew him best. Only in retrospect do we see the amazing qualities he possessed.

The examples of Lincoln and countless other leaders make clear the romantic folly of the "great man" theory of history, which tells us that great individuals—Charlemagne, Napoleon, Winston Churchill, Margaret Thatcher, Indira Gandhi—come along at certain points in history to change the course of events.

The great man theory says that events flow through these individuals to create historical singularities. It's an idea, particularly in an era when the cult of personality is so strong, that many of us have bought in to. Indeed, the "leadership industry" in many ways capitalizes on our romantic fascination with the great man theory. As a result, many leadership books read as instruction manuals on how to become great. Real leadership just isn't like that. Leaders aren't heroes—and they're not always men.

Lyricist Stephen Sondheim (1964), in his musical *Anyone Can Whistle*, powerfully tackles the subject of leadership and our tendency to romanticize it. His song "There Won't Be Trumpets" reminds us that our leaders are human, and warns: "*There won't be trumpets or bolts of fire / To say he's coming.*"

Sondheim is of course correct. Leaders *don't* appear in a flash of lightning, and the pedestal on which we insist on placing them is often, like their feet, made of clay.

More importantly, though, when we argue that leadership is not a single magical quality, but rather a diverse and *situational* collection of practical competencies, we leave the door open for luck—which, again, is an important element. Luck and timing are more crucial than we want to admit. As competent as any leader may be, bad luck and poor timing will prove insurmountable obstacles. "Better to be lucky than smart," said a wise person.

The evolutionary approach of biodynamics teaches us that leadership, as with any quality that provides an organism with a Darwinian advantage, can only be selected for within the context of specific environmental conditions. Lee Iacocca emerged from a Ford Motor Company that, to put it mildly, could not make use of his skill set. But he found a home at Chrysler that allowed him to flourish. Likewise, it may well be that Jack Welch, at this writing considered among the greatest corporate leaders of all time, would have been an anonymous functionary in a company that did not provide him the opportunities of a General Electric.

The list goes on, in political history and in the corporate world, of men and women who recognized and seized opportunities to use their capabilities and became distinguished leaders—and that is what has been misunderstood. These men and women, biodynamically speaking, became leading parts of systems in which their particular qualities were not only welcomed, but *needed*. Their leadership happened naturally and spontaneously.

The hierarchical principle of biodynamic theory says that leadership is a naturally occurring characteristic of complex systems. Leaders emerge from social and organizational contexts that require them. Some natural leaders just happen to have the personality, skill set, or background to fit a situation. Others, maybe those a bit more worthy of admiration, see an opportunity and somehow transform themselves into the right person for the job—reminiscent of the myth of Proteus. But the role of chance and timing should not be underestimated as we look more closely at some of the more common myths of leadership.

The Renaissance Person Myth

Another myth that we cherish about our great leaders is what I call the Renaissance person myth—that all leaders are multitalented geniuses. It is as if the collective *needs* to view its leaders in a worshipful way and demands that they be good at everything. Aside from being impossible, this expectation is an unfair burden on the leader.

Former President Bill Clinton taught us that you can be a political genius without being a particularly strong moral leader. One could perhaps say the same of Thomas Jefferson—a great head of state and Founding Father, yet a slaveholder and a spendthrift as well. Or one might point to John F. Kennedy, whom millions thought of as an exemplar of character, only to find out decades later that he simply wasn't.

In reality, we should only expect our leaders to have the right skill set at the right time, and to make the right short- and long-term decisions given the organization (the system) in which they are operating. Anything more verges on idolatry.

Pertinent here is the fact that, while great leaders are often very intelligent and indeed gifted, a leader must above all have the ability to *focus to be truly successful*. It is the gift of concentration that, in my observation, differentiates successful leaders from unsuccessful ones.

The greatest leaders also have a gift for understanding complex systems in ways that very few other people do. They intuit the axioms outlined in Part I of this book. The most adept leaders have a particular grasp of the integral principle—an almost instinctive understanding of the ways in which systems can be broken down and combined, as well as of the inherent parameters of a viable system. Having this knowledge, leaders can use the system to their advantage.

Extremely adept political leaders use state and national parties to win elections; a corporate leader uses divisions and functions to create business success. This particular genius has, in my experience, been underrated, but it will become more important as systems grow in complexity over time, and as we all become more a part of the fourth kingdom.

A subsidiary point within the Renaissance person myth is the notion that the smartest person will inevitably end up in a leadership position. Once we understand the theory of multiple intelligences—that there are differing *kinds* of genius (Gardner, 1983)—we see that different gifts will be successful in different cases. A leader *once* is not necessarily a leader *always*.

Take the example of Dwight David Eisenhower. His analytic intelligence on a military level was what allowed him to win the Battle of the Bulge. But did he possess, later, the interpersonal intelligence that would enable him to be the most successful leader of the free world? Most historians would say no.

The interpersonal qualities that made Lyndon Johnson so successful as a politician in his early years may have hampered his ability to lead the country during the Vietnam crisis. Johnson was a shrewd manipulator of people but seemed to lack a larger strategic vision, at least on the international front.

In the end, the Renaissance person myth does a disservice because it oversimplifies the role of leader, implying that a leader can do all things. In fact, from the biodynamic perspective, complex systems require *multiple*, often completely *differentiated* roles involving multiple players in order to make the system work. The leader is merely one cog in the wheel, albeit a key one.

The Instant Recognition Myth

That leaders are somehow instantly recognizable is another key myth. Leaders are not always obvious or apparent. In fact, they're not always recognized as great until well after the fact. Perhaps even more interesting, many never appeared to be great leaders even to themselves.

In his book *Good to Great* (2001), Jim Collins notes that Level V leadership—the highest level in his particular scheme—is an odd mixture of humility and fierce resolve. Great corporate leaders in his study often avoided the limelight and rarely portrayed themselves or felt comfortable being characterized as the great leaders they actually were. It was only looking back, years later, that one could see how much value these great corporate leaders had brought to their companies, and how successful they really were compared to their peers.

This long-term view brings up the importance of persistence. The idea of instant success is part of the leadership mythology, and it is absurd. Real-life battles are often won through a combination of strategy, tactics, timing, luck, and other factors. The victories aren't always dramatic, and sometimes they seem to take forever.

A great leader instinctively knows this—or simply doesn't care—and perseveres.

The Sagacity Myth

The sagacity myth is my name for the notion that a great leader follows a preordained destiny to greatness—that success for some is inevitable. What manifest destiny is to political states, preordination is to corporate leadership—and it is equally presumptuous. Based once again on romantic fantasies, the sagacity myth implies that our leaders are all-wise and all-knowing. Not only does the leader know what to do at every turn, there is in fact only one true path, the secrets of which they alone are privy to.

The reality? Leaders, even the best, don't always know what to do, and there often isn't just one path or solution. Axiom 7, the synthetic principle, reminds us that the world is fundamentally chaotic and unpredictable. The idea of a single solution to anything is a gross oversimplification at best. In complex systems and environments there are almost always multiple paths, and more than one set of solutions to any challenge that presents itself.

Our naive, childish idea of an infallible, all-knowing leader must be replaced by a more mature, practical conception of a leader who will wisely consider multiple choices, seek intelligent counsel, keep options open, and choose the most viable course of action.

Romantic? No. Practical? Yes.

Leaders are not heroes, though we tend to imbue them with many of the characteristics of literary, historical, or religious figures. We are programmed from fairy tales onward to see the world in a narrative way. As a result, we tend to impose a dramatic arc on our leaders and view them as otherworldly archetypes—simultaneously heroes, "good kings," and beneficent parental figures.

Making the Complex Too Simple

All of these myths do the same thing—they make it possible for us to oversimplify something that is inherently complex. They have all done and are continuing to do a disservice, not only to individuals aspiring to be leaders, but also to the very organizations and systems that need those leaders to function effectively. When we buy into these myths, we are setting ourselves up for disappointment. Indeed, between the writing and editing of this chapter, Jack Welch has gone from a corporate god to an "oh how the mighty are fallen" morality play. I can't help but wonder if Welch wouldn't have fallen quite so far had he not bought into the very mythologies discussed in this chapter.

We must remember that the best leaders are not "instant," but emerge organically from the systems in which they are cultivated. In fact, I would suggest that the instant recognition myth has probably done more to hurt corporate America than any other misconception.

In the boom times of the 1990s, leaders were expected to be successful—unreasonably, dramatically successful—in a relatively short time frame. This expectation was exacerbated by the fact that some few did indeed, at least during the dot-com era, seem to meet those unrealistic expectations. Recent events in the post-dot-com world have shown us once again that the truly great leaders are the ones with staying power. The problem with leaders who emerge quickly is that they often flame out just as quickly. With instant recognition often comes a precipitous fall from grace.

Infinitely preferable is an organic view, in which leaders emerge from the context of everyday business challenges, and are not expected to be anything other than the right person at the right place and time.

What Leaders Need to Do

That the best leaders do not need to be told what to do is yet another myth—which is the reason for the following prescriptions to present and future leaders:

Embrace complexity

Organizations are complex and are becoming ever more so, as are the ways in which they thrive and grow. Leaders need to understand this, appreciate it, and act accordingly. Despite our primitive psychological need for simple answers and easy solutions, leaders cannot be entrapped by such simplifications. The world is a complex of complex systems—and even if no one else understands and accepts that fact, our leaders must.

Appreciate people

The essential element of any organization is the people that comprise it. We occasionally fall into the trap, by speaking about systems abstractly, of forgetting that they consist of human beings. Implied, of course, in the appreciation of *people* is the appreciation of *oneself*—as a person, as a complex system interacting with other complex systems, and as a component and vital part of a yet-larger system. A good leader must be able to understand people, empathize with them, and demonstrate emotional as well as cognitive strategic leadership, as Daniel Goleman (1998) has articulately demonstrated in his work on emotional intelligence. Along with that, a leader must know his or her own mind and must not fall prey to the traps of immediately gratifying simple needs and pathological pleasures.

Manage information

Information management is quickly becoming the most essential aspect of competent leadership. The leader must be positioned to take in information, process it, then output the data in a form by which the whole system is to be managed. In other words, a new way to see leadership is as an information nexus in a complex system.

7

IF IT ONLY HAD A BRAIN: THE NEW CORPORATE GOVERNANCE

The More Things Change

What do corporate boards of directors do? The world has changed in the information age. Methods of doing business have changed and management's responsibilities have changed, so how has the role of boards changed?

First, in some ways boards of directors haven't changed at all. It has always been the responsibility of corporate boards to represent the ownership of a company. Yes, board members may offer star power and celebrity status in some cases, as well as other intangibles. But their functions are primarily to approve corporate philosophies and missions; to oversee, monitor, and evaluate corporate directions; to review strategies and business plans; and to weigh in on financial objectives and progress. Ultimately, one could say that a board of directors is responsible for thinking and looking ahead—for helping to assess, plan, and provide stewardship.

In the last quarter century, directors have been of four types. There are high-level managers—for example, CEOs from other companies, who have or have had similar responsibilities in their own organizations. There are individuals who represent financial interests and expertise, often by virtue of ownership in the company. There are, for lack of a better term, figureheads: celebrities, or individuals who fulfill real or imagined quotas of gender, race, age, or special interest. Finally, there are content experts, such as the biologists and physicians on the board of Merck or the electronics engineers and professors on the board of Intel.

Recent Evolution

At one point in our history—going all the way back to the original East India Company—an organization's board was its ownership, and the board hired managers to run things. Then in the last three or four decades, with the advent of professional management, "inside managers" began taking over the jobs that boards used to do. Boards devolved into simple rubber stamps for the activities of managers.

In addition, as organizations grew in complexity and as economies went from merely multinational to truly global, the world became far too complex for the typical part-time director. The job of director became bigger, without a subsequent change in the way the job was carried out or in the way it was filled and remunerated.

The information revolution introduced further challenges, because inside directors—including company CEOs—were suddenly enables to know and control all or much of the pertinent company information. Outside directors rarely had the time, and almost never had the access, to review much of the data that was required to keep them well or even adequately informed.

Information Please

In the modern commercial organization, the amount of information flowing at any given moment is incomprehensibly large. Most Fortune 50 companies have the financial infrastructures of small countries. This means that someone who is not intimately involved in the day-to-day details of corporate management has a difficult time remaining knowledgeable about what's really going on. Boards of directors are analogous to the elected leadership of such small countries. The difference is they have much less direct power and ability to impact the system.

In recent years, corporations have often combined the role of CEO and chairman of the board, concentrating power in the hands of the CEO. Although there's some evidence of this trend abating, it nevertheless represents a disturbing direction; it assumes that since companies have become so complex, life is simpler with one person in control. While this is perhaps true in some instances and in some ways, it is an unrealistic fantasy to believe that one person is always going to act in a manner that is in everyone's interest—a benevolent dictator, operating without appropriate checks and balances. Certainly, the abuses that have come to light in the early years of this decade [NB: this essay was written in 2002] have been aided and abetted by a political structure and climate of absolute power at the top.

In the contemporary organization, this is perhaps where the board of directors' most important new role comes in: as a key part of a system of checks and balances. But what, exactly, are they checking and balancing?

The Brain

Consider the metaphor of the brain as a complex system. For this purpose, think of the brain as a leading part of the system, corresponding to Axiom 4, the hierarchical principle of DST. The human brain evolved pleasure centers in its more primitive regions. These pleasure centers are what Freud called the id. It is only with the evolution of the ego and the superego (or, in biophysiological terminology, the *neocortex*), that human beings can overlay a reality principle on the pleasure principle, to keep us from constantly acting on immediate impulse. Just as the ego and superego override the id within the human mind, a corporate board of directors must override the need for corporate pleasure— i.e., for immediate fiscal gratification.

In the early part of our current century, the pleasure principle ruled in corporate America. The desire for immediate gratification ran unchecked in corporations like Enron, Tyco, Global Crossing, Adelphia, and WorldCom (all now footnotes in business history since the original publication of this book). As I write this, corporate America is in the throes of transition. Will a higher standard of behavior emerge, enforced by boards of directors?

Let's continue the brain metaphor a bit further.

Evolutionary theory teaches us that the human brain evolved from a primitive neural transmission system to greater complexity, culminating in the current sophistication of the human central nervous system. (See Axioms 3 and 4.)

As with simple biological organisms, simple businesses involve small numbers of simple processes. But as business organizations grow and become more complex, they need a management structure, in the same way more sophisticated organisms require a central nervous system. In human evolution, increased activity required the central nervous system to evolve to enable the brain to plan, to develop hunting strategies, and to keep increasingly complex data at the ready. Similarly, in the evolution of organizations, the business's "brain," i.e., management, must develop to accommodate a corporation's increasing complexity.

In the human brain, the prefrontal lobes of the neocortex are the most recently evolved regions. It is this area of the brain, with its many folds and resulting large surface area, which "makes us human." The brain stem, sometimes called the primitive brain, is the earlier-evolved portion responsible for reflexive functions like respiration and heartbeat. A bit more evolved area, though still quite primitive, is the limbic system or so-called reptilian brain—the true center of Freud's pleasure principle and the seat of our impulses for instant gratification.

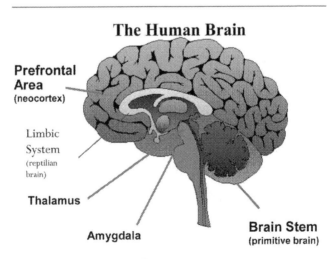

Figure 7-1

Completing the comparison with business, then, let's admit that contemporary corporations are either stuck in or have devolved to the reptilian brain. Business has been lobotomized, if you will—it has regressed to an earlier, more primitive state in which immediate fiscal gratification rules the day. Any television viewer watching the steady parade of fallen executives before congressional hearings—particularly a viewer who was a stockholder in any of those executives' companies—would be hard-pressed, I think, to disagree.

Leadership

If this is the current state of the business world, what then is the function of leadership in such organizations? I suggest that the primary function of leadership is to acknowledge the nature of systems and to acknowledge their biodynamic complexity.

The growing popularity of enterprise resource planning systems (ERPs) within corporations is a perfect example of this growing complexity. A literal manifestation of the differentiation principle (Axiom 3), ERPs have become the core of the central nervous system of many of today's largest organizations. These systems are increasingly necessary to manage and lead.

But back to boards of directors—who is the ideal board member in such a business environment? Today's ideal board member must have an area of content- related or functional expertise. An ideal director of Pepsi-Cola, for example, might be a chemist who understands sugar molecules and their role in soft drinks. Another example might be a person with particular expertise in a general business area—say, executive compensation, procurement, or transportation.

Minimum tickets for entry to boards of directors include motivation, interest, critical-thinking skills, rough knowledge of the industry, and general intelligence. Devoid of content-related or functional knowledge of some kind, a director sitting on a board is merely a figurehead. Many of the former four-star generals and high-level politicians who populate corporate boards are exactly that.

A director's real job is to carry the banner of the reality principle, as an antidote to the instant financial gratification and success that inside managers increasingly promise, yet less often deliver. In retrospect, the Internet bubble was the tulipomania of our age. The speculative frenzy was not the cause of greed but only its efflorescence. As corporate "lifers" watched twentysomethings become instantly wealthy, they wanted what they perceived as their fair share. The gloves came off, caution was thrown to the wind, and everyone waded into the swamp to grab what was "rightfully" theirs.

Ten years before, Gordon Gecko in the movie *Wall Street* had told his audience, "Greed is good." The rising tide raised all boats. Sure, CEOs and insiders got rich, but so did everyone else, and that made greed okay. Except the temptation for the wolf guarding the lambs proved too great, and excesses became inevitable. Now it is time for the pendulum to swing back to the more reasonable center (see Chapter 14 in this volume).

Inside v. Outside

The inside v. outside tension of many corporate boards has various ramifications. Historically, no one on a typical board was an inside director. As the role of management became more professionalized, managers were invited to sit in the boardroom. This created a dichotomy of interests by which internal board members were disproportionately rewarded as a result of their actions. It fell to the outside directors—who truly must represent all the stakeholders—to hold the line.

Nowhere is this function more observable than on the compensation committee, where outside directors have traditionally been expected to prevent insiders from rewarding themselves with ridiculously large salaries and bonuses. Recently this function seems to have collapsed, and many boards have lost their way.

Let's look briefly at two groups that make up typical boards, and see exactly what they offer.

The first group is executives from other companies. They often bring a working knowledge of business, both on the financial side and on the organization/infrastructure side. They also bring their network of relationships and their social capital, which are helpful, even critical, for the company to do business. For example, Fred might be the CEO of Company Y, which makes widgets, and he's on the board of Company X. A top salesperson of Company X has been trying to reach someone at Company Y to get a good deal on widgets. Fred can be instrumental in cutting through a bureaucratic maze to get the deal done. This scenario would be a typical and totally justifiable way for directors to contribute to the functioning of a company.

The second group consists of owners with a variety of interests. As directors, they have a responsibility to act in the best long-term interest of the company.

Actions that may be profitable in the short run but not in the long run should be avoided where possible. This, of course, runs counter to a market economy that grades companies based on quarterly performance. Investors who seek short-term gains must be aware that the long term counts too. Short-term profits, when they increase shareholder value, may be defensible, but these short-term profits often come at the expense of long-term market position. Steering the company through this delicate balancing act is part and parcel of responsible board leadership.

A Board's Functional Nature

If a corporation is an organism—a bioeconomic entity that uses capital and information to sustain itself, and whose elements all have a function—what is the functional nature of a corporation's board of directors? (See Figure 7-2.)

We need to go back to the subjects of complexity and differentiation. Organizations have become so complex that one person, even one group of people, cannot handle the full executive functioning of the business. Management and governance are separate tasks, even though they are certainly complementary. As these tasks differentiate, boards and management will invariably develop in different directions according to somewhat different agendas. It is the dynamic tension between the agendas of management and the agendas of governance that will inevitably lead to the most fruitful conversations.

On an ideal board, men and women with specific areas of structural expertise will complement those with expertise in the core competencies, products, and services of the

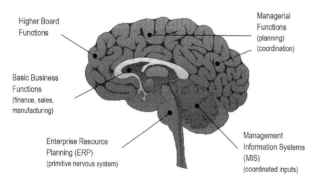

Figure 7-2: The Corporate Brain

company. These individuals will in turn complement board members with expertise in capital (an investment banker, for instance). And these members will, in their turn, all be complemented by a randomized element giving the board a connection to the world in ways that are not necessarily linear or straightforwardly anticipatable—members of minority or special interest groups, for example, or celebrity figureheads with a legitimate point of view. (See Figure 4-2 for a graphic representation of the corporate landscape.)

Why would all these disparate voices be desirable? Because the board must be a place that synthesizes multiple inputs from a wide array of information sources—the wider the better. If an information economy stands for anything, it stands for the need to stay as current as possible in a world that is constantly in flux.

Then and Now

As the modern organization evolved in the 1950s, a gray-flannel-suited class of professional managers came to control the organization. Board members were marginalized. Now, we see that the pendulum has swung too far in that direction. Boards have become overmarginalized. Managers for whom absolute power has corrupted absolutely, and who in some cases have used the company as their own personal cash register, have eclipsed boards' executive and oversight functions.

It's all part of the same malaise—the organization has become too complex, and professional managers are the only ones with the resources of time, money, infrastructure, and access to be able to fully manage the company. The fox is running the henhouse. With the debacles of Enron, Worldcom, Adelphia, and Arthur Andersen, we realize that the status quo, in which managers have almost exclusive responsibility for the way a company is run, must come to an end.

Biologists tell us that evolution occurs in fits and starts; it is safe to assume that the evolution of corporations and of their boards should proceed in the same manner. The level of comfort that was the price directors paid for allowing managers to have their way with companies must be rethought. If an organization trades on information, and indeed subsists on information, then we have to recognize that directors must participate in this rich flow of information to bring value to the company. This certainly has not been the case up to the present time.

Information systems have evolved along with the modern organization. The IT infrastructure has become the means by which managers have gained and maintained control of the organization. For directors to have a chance at parity, they must be able to access the same information. Knowledge is indeed power in the corporate arena, as everywhere else. The new corporate director will have and be able to use information tools never before available, and will be able to make decisions that are informed to a degree never before possible.

So does all of this change the nature of who is appointed to boards? Should it? Yes and yes—although the change may be gradual rather than dramatic.

We begin to have some insight, grounded in dynamic systems theory, of what board members need to know in order to contribute. They need to add value in at least one of the functional areas already discussed. They need a portfolio of expertise and accomplishment. They need to offer a commitment to increasing their own human capital, both in the areas in which they already claim expertise and in areas into which they may want to expand.

And they must be informed and committed to staying informed on an ongoing basis.

In Summary

"If I only had a brain!" lamented the scarecrow in *The Wizard of Oz*. The scarecrow's lament echoes in the listless performance of boards of directors throughout the business world. Board seats, once doled out to good old boys like country club memberships, have often been a reflection of a desire to maintain the status quo, to rubber-stamp the policies of a CEO. As evidence, note the trend in recent years to consolidate the CEO and chairman roles, with the board performing perfunctory oversight when it does anything at all.

In the last several decades, companies have grown so big and so complex that coordinating information necessary to manage them has become a major corporate function. Modern management requires modern information technology, and the ubiquitousness of ERP providers like SAP and Oracle attests to this fact.

Yet while the past decade has seen an explosion of information technology available to management, boards have been left deaf, dumb, and blind. Until quite recently, the board was almost entirely dependent on the CEOs and managers over whom they had oversight responsibilities for the information required to evaluate performance. Yes, there were the accountants, but recent events have shown how easily they can be manipulated. The sad truth is that modern knowledge management technology has not yet reached the board. And this must change.

A number of technologies, services, and knowledge management solutions are converging to solve the boards' dilemma of lack of independent sources of information. The ability to provide solutions for the knowledge needs of directors is about to change the face of corporate governance. No longer will directors lurch from quarterly meeting to quarterly meeting, playing catch-up the night before when they receive an information packet as thick as a small telephone book. In the company of the future, directors will be plugged in, receiving real-time streaming data pushed to their desktops that reflects corporate performance, competitive intelligence, and just about anything else they need to carry out their responsibilities.

8

FROM SHIRTSLEEVES TO SHIRTSLEEVES: THE INEVITABLE RISE AND FALL OF FAMILY BUSINESSES

I once attended a conference for family businesses at which a sociologist said, "There's no such thing as an entrepreneur—there are only entrepreneurial families."

What she meant by this, I learned, was that behind every successful businessperson is a family that supports that person every step of the way. We can all bring to mind stories of business startups in which the entrepreneur is out in the field doing deals while his wife, baby on one knee, does the company's bookkeeping at the kitchen table; or the building contractor whose college-age kids don tool belts to work at construction sites during school vacations.

True entrepreneurialism, my colleague was saying, is a family matter, not an individual phenomenon. If entrepreneurs are the engines of capitalism that we're constantly being told they are, then families are the pistons that provide power to those engines. Family support enables entrepreneurial success.

I think my colleague had another, more subtle point that is consistent with a leadership myth highlighted in a previous chapter. The entrepreneur as the Lone Ranger or a knight errant going out to conquer the world alone is one of the mythic tales of capitalism. While I do think the accomplishments of entrepreneurs are heroic, rarely do they accomplish their tasks alone. Save for a few stories like *The Swiss Family Robinson*, we rarely speak of heroic families. Perhaps we should do so more.

It is rare to find an entrepreneur who has not brought family into play in some way. Support is crucial. Add to that the need to form groups in which values are shared, a common heritage is referenced, and a common worldview reigns, and we have all the components for a successful family enterprise. From Saddam Hussein to Tony Soprano, families are considered more trustworthy, especially in authoritarian cultures. We even see this phenomenon in religion, as demonstrated by the Catholic Medici and Borgia popes and the Jewish Hasidic courts of Eastern Europe. Indeed, the Cohanim and Levites of Judaism, based on early tribal affiliations dating back to Moses, may be the most ancient surviving hereditary occupational roles still extant.

In Part I of this book, we discussed systems theory and the concept of *leading parts* in those systems. If small or start-up businesses are complex systems, then entrepreneurs are certainly their leading parts, whether those systems are family businesses or not. The entrepreneur is the person who surveys the business landscape and sees or intuits a void to be filled. The entrepreneur is the agent, the catalyst, and the filler of unfilled niches in his fourth kingdom domain, in the same way that an organism in a natural ecosystem fills a niche in the local food chain.

In both cases, what's happening is a calibrating of forces or energy in the system. Successful new organisms in an ecosystem find untapped resources and a way to exploit those resources successfully. Similarly, entrepreneurs find a way to exploit previously untapped resources in the business ecosystem. Like a seed crystal in a vat, an entrepreneur is the element around which the business crystallizes and grows.

Do entrepreneurs *remain* the leading parts of their systems? The answer is no in most cases, considering that the average business only survives about twenty-five years. Most businesses do not survive beyond the life of their founder. So when the founder of a family business retires and that business evolves, it typically becomes more than a family business; it is simply a business. True, that business will develop *other* leading parts—the tenth CEO of a multinational corporation is as much a leader as the founder, and there are many CEOs who have built the brand well beyond the founder. But the role of founding entrepreneur is unique. While there are founding entrepreneurs who do not start family businesses, there are few family businesses that do not begin with a founding entrepreneur.

Family businesses are fascinating and unique denizens of the fourth kingdom. I have had interesting experiences consulting to family businesses that reinforce my observations. For the purposes of this discussion, I define family businesses as those organizations in which (a) a single family has effective control over decisions, (b) members view the business as a family asset, and (c) they are committed to maintaining control of those assets into the future.

It is of course a mistake to think of family businesses as necessarily being small. Some studies show that 37% of *Fortune 500* companies are family-controlled, whether shareholders know it or not. Family businesses represent the fastest-growing sector of the economy, as well as a considerable percentage of all new job creation. Such businesses, by some measures, represent more than 50% of the gross domestic product. And these numbers apply only to the U.S. economy. Outside the United States, the percentages are even higher. Family businesses are big business in Europe, Asia, and Africa.

From an evolutionary point of view, family businesses are most likely the earliest form of business. If our evolutionary economics analysis is correct, *family farms* in agrarian societies were probably the very first family businesses—indeed the very first *businesses.*

The shift from family to family business entailed a more complex differentiation of roles and responsibilities split among family members. Evolutionarily speaking, it is only a small jump from these family farms to other types of family businesses based on crafts and trades like milling and baking.

Today, family businesses are a robust form of commerce in virtually every imaginable industry. Robust, yes. But stable? I think not.

Through my own study of family businesses over the years, I have developed what I call a *bipolar theory* of these organizations. This theory proposes that family businesses are inherently unstable, and that the tendency is either to revert to a simple, nonbusiness family or to develop into a full-scale business organization. It is difficult and unusual to be able to be both simultaneously.

The reality of family businesses is that, at least in modern times, only about 30% of them survive a first-generation transition. In fact, fewer than 10% of family businesses ever survive into the third generation of management. There is an expression in at least five different languages that communicates something akin to the English-language expression, "Shirtsleeves to shirtsleeves in three generations." Embedded in the phrase is the recognition that family businesses are, from a multigenerational perspective, unstable, and consequently almost never long-lived. Family psychology illuminates why this is so.

The very drives that propel an entrepreneur to launch a business— financial deprivation, lack of social status, need for security, compulsion to prove oneself—are, if the entrepreneur is successful, no longer present in the family's second generation. The heirs begin functioning from a completely different set of needs. The interpersonal dynamics of the two generations are distinct, and the third generation is even farther from the first. Changes tend to stabilize in the fourth or fifth generations, though by this time they will have lost many of their unique family qualities.

The bipolar theory paradoxically states that to survive, a family business must stop being a family business. That is, in the long term, you can be a *family* or you can be a *business*—but you can't be both well.

There are rare exceptions to this generalization, but these are the exceptions that prove the rule. The Henokiens, for example, is a somewhat secret society—a kind of hyperelite private club— of family businesses. To be eligible for membership, a company must be over 200 years old, run by the founders' descendants, have the majority of capital held by the original family, and be in good financial health. There are only about thirty member families in the Henokiens, scattered throughout Europe and Asia. It may in fact be the most exclusive club in the world, and my hunch is that its membership isn't growing rapidly. Yes, there's the Gekkeikan Sake Company, which has been brewing sake in Japan for 360 years, or the Sarret family, who have been hoteliers for over 600 years—but they are emphatically not the norm (see www.henokiens.com).

These companies have no doubt learned things about succession and continuity that would be the envy of larger businesses. I suspect their typically small size and insular nature are correlated with their longevity, in the same way that the tallest tree in the forest is usually not the oldest. However, their status as a small, elite group meeting in semisecret at various places around the world suggests a fragile existence.

What are the ramifications of this inherent instability in family businesses? Family business consulting is a niche consulting market for attorneys, accountants, insurance professionals, money managers, and organizational consultants. However, if the goal of the family business consultant is to keep the family business alive at all costs (and this is not necessarily what all of these consultants try to do), does the bipolar theory suggest that family business consulting is an exercise in futility? Let's look at the problem, not from the perspective of family dynamics, but from the perspective of shareholder capitalism.

The core tenet of shareholder capitalism is that a company is managed on behalf of all its shareholders equally, in accordance with their proportion of ownership. Yet family businesses set in motion a dynamic which creates a multitiered system in which some shareholders, i.e., family members, are advantaged over others, independent of ownership. Hence the inherent structural instability of a family business. If family members are the sole owners, this eliminates one source of friction, but neither is this classic shareholder capitalism. I suspect that the ability and willingness to limit ownership to family members is one secret of the successful Henokien companies.

One can point to families that have been able to sustain a strong identity through the ages; family pride can run deep. Even in a country as young as the United States, we have families that put great stock in tracing their bloodlines to the *Mayflower* or the Sons and Daughters of the American Revolution. The family of Abraham Lincoln's assassin, John Wilkes Booth, is today a tightly cohesive group on a mission to restore their notorious ancestor's "good name." But those are families, not family *businesses*.

I suggest that most successful businesses that started as family concerns are, in fact, not family businesses at all anymore; rather, they have transformed into full-fledged non-family-dominated corporations—even if, as in the case of such companies as Marriott, W. R. Grace, or Hershey, they still carry the name of a founder.

Hershey is actually an interesting case. Among the most positive aspects of successful family businesses is a strong commitment to a set of values beyond the profit motive. A well-managed family business has very high loyalty among its employees for this reason.

These values may, in the best success stories, survive beyond the founder, and even the family. So when the Hershey Company, a positive force in the rural Pennsylvania town where it is based, contemplated selling themselves to an international candy concern, there was a huge backlash from workers, townspeople, and even some of the directors. The values that Hershey represented were by now part of the fabric, and of course the economy, of the town and the region.

The case of Bergdorf-Goodman, the luxury New York retailer, is another interesting family business case study. The founder, a true entrepreneur and retail genius from an impoverished immigrant background, was an enormous success.

His son, however, grew up ensconced in an extremely wealthy lifestyle and spent his adult life as a *bon vivant* and dilettante. The son continued to be associated with the business, but he was clearly not the commercial engine his father had been—nor could he be, by temperament or inclination.

Now, in the third and fourth generations, we see a family of substantial wealth that is completely without ties to any retail venture. Bergdorf-Goodman is thriving—but as a business, not as a *family* business.

The Kennedys have evolved from a successful business family to a political dynasty. The Rockefellers went a similar route. Neither family has remained an actual family business.

Some of the more successful long-term family business ventures have been in the realm of trusts and foundations. Here the family transforms or transports family wealth, obtained from the business, into a new entity called the family trust or foundation. Family foundations may represent a new form or species of the fourth kingdom. Neither businesses nor religions, they tend to be values based—or to use a new term, *ideotropic*. That is, they use a shared set of values to guide the activities of the group.

Americans tend to be aggressively egalitarian in their business outlook, and perhaps for that reason, in some ways we chafe at the reality of family businesses. As a fact of business life, family businesses have been much more readily accepted in Europe and Asia than in America. Whether we're talking about the Rothschilds, the Agnellis (Fiat), or the French sportswear empire of Bernard Lacoste, with his crocodile-logo tennis shirts, family businesses are perhaps *the* signal fact of European business life.

Family businesses, then, are among the earliest types of fourth kingdom organisms. They are relatively primitive from an organizational point of view, and are inherently unstable, since they are always either being dragged backward into being "just plain" families or morphing into more standard, sophisticated, nonfamilial business organizations.

Family businesses may be primitive because role differentiation tends to be incomplete and unstable. There is a consistent, abiding uncertainty related to what can be expected from whom in which role. While a family business that ultimately fails because it doesn't evolve into a nonfamily corporation may be unsuccessful in terms of longevity, it may nevertheless have been quite successful in its ability to provide admirably for the family and others for many years.

Biodynamic systems theory offers some interesting clues as to why family businesses are inherently unstable and often fail. Remember that the second axiom focuses on boundaries and their role in maintaining viable systems. Just as the poet Robert Frost pointed out that good fences make good neighbors, so do good boundaries make viable systems.

The family business becomes unstable in future generations for the simple reason that its boundaries cannot function properly. By the second or third generation, the family system, with descendants, in-laws, and cousins, becomes too unwieldy to function as an integrated whole. Successful, 200-plus-year-old family businesses are the ones with clear rules of membership and clear rules of succession. Everyone knows who is in and who is not, and who will be the next leader. The boundary holds.

On the other hand, when the boundary is too severe and not porous enough, the business quickly becomes anemic without the necessary influx of new talent. The "shirtsleeves to shirtsleeves" phenomenon takes hold, and its inertia creates a death spiral for the organization.

Nevertheless, most family businesses are like societies of single-cell organisms that come together in colonies and function as pseudo-organisms—loose aggregations that may or may not become functional wholes. Whether in a family business or in a colony of single-celled creatures, no member can quite survive on its own. Think of a family business as you would any system, because it is just that: a complex dynamic made up of disparate, simpler parts that are similar in many ways, yet which fulfill slightly different roles.

This role differentiation—the child who milks the cows, the mother who harvests the vegetables—is the secret of success in family businesses that do function, for however long. It is also the key, as we discuss in later chapters, to any other kind of business organization's success. Differentiation and natural complementarity of roles is leveraged into business value, and hence survival. This is the ultimate key to appreciating the family business as a social, commercial, and biological phenomenon.

9

THE HEALTH OF ORGANIZATIONS

Natural Science and the Illusion of Predictability

The natural sciences have until recently been under the illusion that all things are predictable. It was always a truism among students of physics, chemistry, and molecular biology that, if you know all the variables, you can predict the outcome. Remember Einstein's conviction that "God does not play dice with the universe."

Unfortunately, after Heisenberg punched a hole in this conceit, the ship sank in the sea of chaos theory. Although it is no longer a defining characteristic, prediction still has a venerable place in experimental science. The illusion of predictability predicated on a reductionist view of cause and effect has gone the way of other social myths that may provide temporary comfort but are not necessarily true.

In *historical science*, however, there exists no such grand and comforting assumption. Historical science simply uses the powers of observation and the application of fundamental scientific principles to understand how things have become what they are, without needing to predict future events.

The historical and the reductive must live side by side. Chemical reactions we see in molecular biology may well be predictable through the science of chemistry, but that is several levels below the level of analysis in historical science. We are revisiting the first axiom here, the notion that the natural world exists in nested layers. The predictable chemical reactions by which food is digested becomes the unpredictable event in the general's stomach that changes the course of a war. The level of analysis pertaining to chemical reactions in the stomach is simply less complex than the level that pertains to world politics.

Students of the historical sciences—whether examining the extinction of the dinosaurs or considering the defeat of Napoleon at Waterloo—realize that the real world is too complex to make specific predictions about the outcomes of complex chains of events. For this reason, the historical sciences are decidedly nonreductionist, and this fact takes us from the first axiom all the way to the seventh axiom. In other words, it takes us from emergence to synthesis, where the elements of the world recombine in unpredictable ways. Compare this insight to the logical positivist philosophy that dominated science throughout the twentieth century and promoted predictability as the primary goal of science, giving it an exalted, even naive authority.

Natural History Is Description, Naturally

Traditionally, all of science was an exercise in inductive reasoning and observation. Understanding something—a life form, a natural phenomenon—was in earliest times an exercise in *description*; this was "natural history." But science and the scientific method introduced the notion that understanding was about *analysis*— that is, the breaking down of a phenomenon into its component parts in order to comprehend the whole. It was this way of thinking that led us to seek out the basic particles of the subatomic world. But—surprise!—quantum theory taught us that trying to understand the natural world based on linear predictability was absurdly reductive and of questionable utility.

Of what relevance is this to the affairs of the fourth kingdom? Well, could anyone have predicted that a small, insignificant, semifurry creature of the Jurassic period would someday control the globe—while the dominant species of that era would roam the earth no more? Historical science helps us to understand, after the fact, how such an apparently unlikely thing could happen. It also helps us to accept that, most of the time, there are simply too many unknowns to predict *any set of complex events* with certainty.

This is true for most if not all fourth kingdom events. Keeping this in mind helps us to avoid the errors of logical positivism made early in the last century by scientists who viewed this kind of inherent predictability not just as a possibility, but as the primary goal of science. While experiments in test tubes and under highly controlled laboratory conditions can yield extremely valuable data, the end results must always be considered in the context of real-life complexities, with the subsequent uncertainty that such extrapolation brings.

Perhaps this is why, in the world of business, so-called reengineering has so often failed: it failed to honor the culture of complexity that coevolved with it. Michael Hammer, among others, has estimated that over 70% of all corporate reengineering efforts end in failure. Simply "reinventing" an organization without understanding the complexity of its evolution up to that point has usually been an exercise in futility. Reengineering is successful only when it convinces an organization that its form must follow function, as in natural evolution. Insight, not engineering, is the key to these successes.

Organizational form is not random. It follows the demands of its environment in the same manner as any biological form. Any aspect of fourth kingdom organisms—like any aspect of biology at large—is best understood at the deepest levels, using the axioms outlined in Part I of this book. Let's look at how the axioms aid us in understanding how organizations work and how they can be improved.

Diagnosing the Organizational Organism

Levels

Levels have to do with the axiom of emergence. *Emergentism* is the philosophy that says that function follows, or emerges from, form. If we really want to understand the various levels of organizational complexity, we have to ask: What is the context of the organization? What is the mission of the company in relation to that context?

Organizations naturally evolve levels as their complexity increases. Levels enable organizations to achieve greater and greater degrees of complex interaction with the environment, without overloading the organization. In examining an organization in this light, the scientist, consultant, executive, or analyst must naturally ask: Are there too many levels? Too few? Is the organizational structure too simple, or too complicated, for the business's needs? The answers to these questions must all relate back to the *purpose* of the organization: Why is it in business, and how can it best accomplish its goals?

Boundaries

In systems theory, *boundaries* relate to the integrity of a system, the importance of identity, and the need to sustain that identity.

Perhaps the most important question around boundaries to ask is: Are the boundaries *functional*?

Remember back to high school biology when you learned that microorganisms were surrounded by semipermeable membranes? These barriers let in outside materials very selectively. Similarly, organizations that swim in the sea of information must take in information selectively. If they are overbounded, not enough information gets in, and they become sluggish, unresponsive, and ultimately moribund. If they are underbounded, such organizations allow in too much information, and they become overwhelmed, unfocused, and unstable.

Differentiation

The key to what modern biologists call "fitness" is the ability to adapt to an environment. One of the major accomplishments of life on the planet, of which the fourth kingdom is but one example, is the ability to develop differentiated roles.

In organizations, the ability to sustain multiple, distinct roles— their clarity, their functionality, and their effective interaction— are determinants of organizational health. Here we must ask the questions: Are roles clear? Are they functional? Do they serve a concrete purpose? Are they respected?

Too much role flexibility within an organization means that roles are not clear. An organization can survive with rigid roles, but only if it has the ability to create additional roles as needed. The ability of an organization to create new roles at a rapid pace is yet another index of organizational health. Executives in particular roles should not only be able to describe their roles, but should be able to explain how these differ from other roles, and how their roles contribute to the success of the whole.

Leadership

Leadership refers to the hierarchy inherent in organizational structures. Leadership allows the organization to maximize efficiency and to reap the benefits of coordination. While differentiation is a prerequisite for leadership, leadership is responsible for coordinating the differentiated parts. It permits yet another level of fitness to exist, and at the same time permits the ability to rapidly deploy resources in a focused and coordinated fashion.

Questions around leadership include: Is there meaningful leadership? Even more important, is it recognized as such? Is there a functional chain of command? Is there a clearly understood line of succession? How does the leader lead? Does the leader's style match the organizational culture and environmental requirements? In other words, is the leadership style effective? How could it be more effective?

Work in organizational culture has demonstrated that some cultures thrive in "command-and-control" environments. Large, predictable markets give rise to such cultures. Companies in quickly changing markets seem to do better with a more distributed leadership model, as elaborated in the works of Doug Snyder, Geoffrey Moore, and Daniel Goleman. Questions relating to how leaders negotiate the matching of leadership style to leadership challenges address the subtle requirements of leadership.

Development

Development refers to predictable changes over time, and to an assumed orderliness to these changes. What are the attitudes of an organization toward the idea of change? Is change permitted?

Is it planned and intelligent, or merely stopgap? Is it embraced or is it fought?

In dynamic environments, organizations themselves must be dynamic, and must be capable of evolving accordingly. In the hectic and overheated business markets of the late 1990s, organizations were expected to change on a dime, sometimes literally overnight. Strategic planning was thought to be dead, and business models were changed as regularly as an executive's socks. While we see this in retrospect as an intemperate response to a market bubble, organizations that behaved in this way nevertheless accurately reflected the turbulent environment in which they conducted business.

Growth

Growth relates to what we referred to in Part I as the *autopoietic* principle. Growth is a metabolic-like function in fourth kingdom organisms. It requires interacting with the environment while honoring internal processes and needs. Growth refers to how the system gets its inputs, especially in the forms of information and capital for fourth kingdom organisms. Large amounts of either enable organizations to grow much more quickly. It is up to the leadership to focus upon and process these resources effectively.

The question of when an organism is best served by growing versus splitting up is an issue on the cutting edge of biodynamically informed organizational study. For example, Hewlett Packard, in the late 1990s, split off its testing division into what became Agilent. The testing division, it could be said, was the heart of HP, and it represented the business at its very origin. Soon after, HP embraced its hardware business by merging with Compaq, setting off a corporate governance crisis that it barely survived. When to split, and when to combine—that is the question.

Issues related to development (or to boundaries, as described above) are rarely easy or obvious. For analysts, some of the considerations that arise at this stage are about evaluating the competitive landscape in which a company functions. How does the organization strategize growth vis-à-vis its competition? How do the parts contribute to the functioning of the whole? Should it grow by multiplying parts (i.e., divisions, companies) and acquisition, or should it just let existing ones get bigger? Which parts should be allowed to grow, and which parts to stagnate or perhaps die? Which parts—like Agilent, in the Hewlett Packard case—should be cast off altogether?

Change

Is there room for unplanned change in an organization? This question may be answered by evaluating the looseness or tightness of fit of a company with its environment. An overregulated, highly controlled organization simply doesn't have the ability to rapidly morph into something else if the need arises.

There are some interesting analogies here in the animal kingdom. Compare, for example, the raccoon and the anteater. The anteater is a finely honed machine perfectly suited to an environment in which ants abound. Anteaters, consequently, have evolved a design that enables them to get at those ants in the most efficient manner. In so doing, anteaters have sacrificed teeth, visual acuity, flexible feet, and numerous other things. Should ants disappear through some environmental mishap, we can say with certainty that the anteaters will have a very hard time surviving.

Raccoons, on the other hand, are omnivores, and highly resourceful and adaptable, because they need to be. As any suburban home-dweller with backyard trash cans will attest, raccoons will try eating different foods and attempt a wide variety of strategies in order to sustain themselves. Anteaters have a tight fit to their environment, while raccoons have a loose fit.

The same loose/tight dynamic is true of fourth kingdom organizations, and indeed a too-tight fit with the environment may account for the abbreviated life cycles of some companies. Smith Corona, for example, "should" have been a leader in the personal computing field. As a manufacturer of typewriters, they virtually owned what was to become the word processing market. Yet the company clung to the niche of typewriting, even as word processing on personal computers gained market share. Meanwhile, a tiny startup called Microsoft, with nothing but vision and a few freelance coders, was able to reinvent the industry and take it by storm.

By being small, smart, and entrepreneurial—the raccoons of their market niche—Microsoft was able to prevail. Granted, Microsoft thrived and Smith Corona failed because of a confluence of events, which in all fairness was not really *predictable*. And that brings us back to our original subject.

Planning, Strategic and Otherwise

As biodynamic systems of varying levels of complexity, businesses are fundamentally unpredictable, just like their analogs in the natural world—especially when examined through the lens of historical science.

A scientist can tell you why Napoleon Bonaparte's stomach hurt him, perhaps, but he can never explain fully why Napoleon lost and Wellington won—not to mention explain the ramifications of that fact throughout subsequent European and world history.

Empiricists, of course, argue this point. They'll insist that if you had a strong enough computer, and if you could quantify everything and crunch all the numbers, you could fully understand and accurately predict anything.

Historical scientists counter that one can never know all of the variables that pertain to a given phenomenon. Reality is a complex interaction of *known and unknown* variables; hence outcomes will always be somewhat mysterious and never fully predictable.

So is business similarly unknowable?

The answer is a qualified yes, though I argue that the effort to know the unknowable is not wasted effort. Let's look at what happened to the practice of strategic planning within organizations.

Strategic planning became the pinnacle of corporate activity in the buttoned-down 1960s and 1970s. Corporate planning took the ideas of logical positivism and applied them to business with a vengeance. Toward the end of this era, strategic planning was considered the primary function of the CEO and the ever-growing executive staff. Strategic planning divisions grew out of all proportion to other parts of companies.

Strategic planning departments embodied the linear thinking of the science of an earlier era. As these departments grew, they consumed more corporate resources, snatched head count, and became the stars around which other corporate functions were forced to revolve.

Scores of people were involved in planning outcomes, determining actions, committing resources, and aiming for specified business targets. It could take a year or more to create a single strategic plan for a subsequent year. Once budgets and resources were locked in, there was very little flexibility.

Today, strategic planning, although it still exists, has been relegated to a more sensible level—because in so many cases it was wasted effort. It simply didn't work. In its place, we see the advent of what is sometimes called *visioning*, *futuring*, or *scenario planning*.

The apocryphal story about scenario planning comes from Royal Dutch Shell. In the late 1960s and early 1970s, the company was allegedly concerned that its world was becoming too complex and unpredictable. The corporation decided to create a division of scenario planning, the purpose of which was to extrapolate multiple story lines for the future. What would the world of oil be like at $50 a barrel? At $5 a barrel? What would happen in the event of Soviet dominance, or of a nuclear war? What if the Arabian oilfields were engulfed in flames?

These were not scientific predictions; they were simply narratives. And yet the stories, which fit well with an historical science worldview and method, captured the complexities better than any linear quantitative predictions ever could have. Thus, when war in the Persian Gulf actually broke out following the fall of the shah and the Iranian hostage crisis—when oil did indeed soar to $50 a barrel—Royal Dutch Shell pulled out its scenario and was able to thrive in market conditions for which only it had prepared.

Since that time, scenario planning has become an essential part of corporate planning. It enables companies to exploit trends, to manage unexpected events, and to monitor critical indicators for the purpose of understanding and reacting to dramas playing out in the real world.

The critical phrase here is "real world"—a realm of utter complexity, which is the home of all fourth kingdom organisms. It is not the test tube or laboratory, where, admittedly, great gains were made in a previous era, but which were never real-life homes to any creature, whatever kingdom it inhabited.

10

COEVOLVING WITH ORGANIZATIONS: ON THE RELATIONSHIP OF WORK TO THE FOURTH KINGDOM

The Age of Information Harvesting

I began my excursion into biodynamic theory as a systems psychologist searching for ideas that I could turn into practical guidance for the families and individuals with whom I worked. Such journeys are never straight lines. Thus, although I began writing over ten years ago as a systems-oriented family therapist, I have since evolved into a systems-oriented organizational consultant—perhaps not so large a leap.

As the principal of my own consulting firm, I was able to apply my ideas at the highest levels of organizations, working with CEOs, COOs, CFOs, and boards of directors. I have found that although my clients' needs inform the work I do, biodynamic ideas remain very much in the background. In other words, while the executives with whom I work don't know much about biodynamic theory, and they've never heard me speak of the seven axioms delineated in Part I of this book, the ideas are constantly in my head as I try to apply what I know. My goal? To help executives navigate their extraordinarily complex world.

In the past year or two, I have taken my desire to help one step further. I have joined with several colleagues to create the *Executive Development Corporation (EDC)*, a company dedicated to increasing the value of human capital within organizations of all kinds. (Note for the second edition: In the last decade, EDC morphed into Llesiant, an information services company, which was acquired by the Bureau of National Affairs, which was in turn acquired by Bloomberg Industry Group, an affiliate of Bloomberg, L.P.).

If you've read Part I of this book, you will have a good, basic understanding of biodynamic theory. And if you've read the other essays in Part II of the book, you can see how biodynamic theory carries through to other aspects of corporate and executive life. But what does the theory mean to an executive working at a desk? Why do we need a biodynamic theory of work?

The answer lies in the emergence of *Homo neticus*—the next phase of human evolution, perhaps—a creature that is descended from *Homo sapiens* but interacts with oceans of information on a daily basis and thrives on the overwhelming amount of information available today. *Homo neticus* is a creature of the information web, created by and living off of the vast array of information available to anyone, and especially to those working in business organizations. (See Chapter 13, "Behold *Homo Neticus*.")

Remember, fourth kingdom creatures use information the way creatures in the other kingdoms use simple sugars and proteins. Information is the fuel of the fourth kingdom; it is the fuel of the information age in general. The next evolutionary challenge, as I tried to make explicit elsewhere, is for humanity to find a way to coevolve *with* the fourth kingdom.

This has already started to happen. The industrial age, or the age of machine-aided manufacture, has now yielded to the information age. Ours is an era of machine-aided information husbandry, as it were. The real challenge now becomes how a creature who evolved as a hunter-gatherer on the plains can successfully function in this complex world of information harvesting.

EDC was founded to facilitate this process and, frankly, to make a profit doing so. EDC has several products, but its premier offering is a solution we called EDC Advantage™. EDC Advantage™ delivers information tailored to the work process. In creating it, we had to explore the roles that exist at work, at home, and in modern life in general. We have tried to create a human/machine interface—sometimes called a dashboard—that enables people to plumb the chaotic world of Internet information and pluck out exactly what they need, when they need it.

A Theory of Work

Information devoid of context is noise. The ability to find specific, *contextual* information is paramount for success in the modern world, and for the eventual success of fourth kingdom organisms.

Think how modern organizations generate and consume vast quantities of information. There are entire industries that have emerged simply to move this information along from one station to the next. One could even argue that the professions of law, accounting, and consulting, and whole industries such as media, computing, and banking, exist solely for the purpose of embodying and transferring information. It's not a question of *whether* human beings will coevolve to adapt to the information needs of the fourth kingdom. This in fact has been happening for the past fifty years. It's a question of when and how—although some executives are still in denial of this fact. The legendary Thomas Watson Sr. of IBM at one time predicted that the world would never need more than five or six large computers. Wrong!

The question we posed at EDC was: How do we facilitate the process of coevolution in the fourth kingdom? To answer it, we needed a theory of work. This theory relies heavily on the concept of roles, essential to the functioning of meaning communities, which are the building blocks of the fourth kingdom. The task we set before ourselves was to understand how computer technology could facilitate role enactment and participation in a variety of meaning communities. In other words, what are the salient meaning communities that people need to access and be a part of in their daily lives, and how can we help make that possible?

Core, Culture, Community, Creativity

Our theory of work separates the work process into four quadrants—*core, culture, community, and creativity.*

Core

The *core* represents productive work, and typically corresponds to a job or role within an organization. Core activities are those behaviors that directly create value for a firm or organization, and that generate capital. They are often a function of unique competencies that define the role in a particular organization. The core represents human capital that translates information into knowledge, and effort into income.

When trying to understand the core role, the questions we want to answer are: How do you provide value? What is your job? Who needs your help? From whom do you get help? What information do you regularly access? What do you need to have, in order to be more effective? After answering these questions, EDC builds information-delivery systems that provide tailored streams of information.

Culture

Culture refers to the organized collaboration of the workplace. In a sense, there are two sides to every role. There is the side of a job that represents an individual, the executive, in relation to his or her work, customers, and clients. And then there is the side that represents the person as a participant in a larger organization. This is the culture of work, and it refers to activities that create or reinforce the social dimensions of an organization.

Sometimes called "corporate citizenship," culture refers to the activities that support the values, ethics, philosophy, and ultimate productivity of a firm. Culture is the arena in which one leverages political capital and social networks to add value—to the core work, to the company, and to other aspects of our own and others' lives. The culture of a company connects the job to the rest of the world. In addition, a culture enables economies of scale that add value and create wealth.

Key questions that often arise at the cultural level have to do with company news, policies, and rules that govern membership and behavior, as well as issues of boundary and membership: who's joining, who's leaving, and who's who.

Community

Community is the integration of work, family, social, and professional worlds. It is the world beyond work. The community is comprised of a network of networks—the family network, the network of friends, and additional meaning communities such as church, school, and municipality. Community is a catch-all quadrant for "the rest of one's life," and it represents the seamless integration of all of one's interests. It is also the place where one aims to strike a balance between work and family.

The key questions that one must ask of community members are: With whom do you want to spend time? What are your communities of interest? What do you like to do socially during personal time? How do you connect with friends? How do you stay informed? How do you include your family? Obviously, the community quadrant could become rather complex; however, for the purposes of EDC Advantage™, we try to keep it all contained in one quadrant.

Creativity

Creativity is the area within which one realizes one's unique and individual potential. This is the private side of the self, which for many is the essence of a person. In the age of *Homo neticus*, this quadrant is becoming smaller and smaller.

If we could imagine what it would mean to be a person without connection, independent of all of the social orbits and influences of work, family, and community, this is where the remaining aspect of such a person could live. We might even debate whether the creative self represents the unique intersection of all the many worlds in which a person lives, or whether it is that singular place which is the absence of any role.

Like the kabbalistic notion of the *ein sof* as a description of the godhead, we come to a similar philosophical conundrum with individuals. *Ein sof* literally translates as "the great nothing," and it raises questions: When we peel back all of our social roles, what remains? Is there anything left of the human beyond social roles and interactions?

These questions are not easily resolved. They go to the heart of the philosophy of personality and require a more thoughtful treatment than is within the scope of this book. However, most people have a strong intuitive understanding of what the self is.

The creativity quadrant aims to reinforce an individual's distinctive approach to information, knowledge acquisition, leisure time, and life in general. The things you read, the music you listen to, the "stuff" that touches your soul, are what we emphasize in this quadrant—without taking a stand on what a soul is, or whether it even exists.

The goal was to value the individual and strive to develop and strengthen his or her uniqueness. At EDC, we held the conviction that people can and should develop personally and professionally. The creativity quadrant is the place where they can focus on doing that. This is the place to care for and tend to one's essence, independent of other demands.

Some of the key questions that need to be answered for consideration of this quadrant are: What do you want to learn? How can you improve? What are your interests? How will you become what you want to be? When do you expect to get there? What are the steps along the way? The information in this quadrant corresponds to what some psychologists refer to as human potential.

The EDC Process

There are three aspects to the process of determining how an individual populates the quadrants. The first is an assessment or information audit. It is as formal as a survey or as impromptu as the question, "What do you need to know?" Through it, we seek to learn the executive's answers to some of the questions posed above.

If you are the executive in question, then for the core, we need to understand the work processes that relate to your job. In culture, we need to know what the organization is about and how it communicates its values and expectations to its members. In community, we need to know who you want to connect with and how. And in creativity, we give you the information you need to begin developing your potential.

Following the information-gathering phase, we provide the means by which to populate the quadrants. That is, it's our job to make available the raw information and tools that enable you to transform information into meaningful knowledge—both to do your job and to live your life.

Finally, it is our responsibility to make certain that the information is current, that it is the best in its class, and that the technology is fully enabled to get what you need, when you need it.

While originally conceived as a desktop solution at work, we have no doubt that ultimately our work process solutions will follow people into their homes, onto their PDAs, and into their cars via cell phones—since that suits (as we have seen) the ubiquitous nature of the information needs of *Homo neticus.*

EDC is tooling up *Homo neticus*—creating the means by which human beings will fully participate as a key fourth kingdom organism.

The evolutionary leap to *Homo neticus* may not yet be proved by physical evidence, but it will likely result in expansion of the prefrontal lobe of the brain in reaction to the need to process increasing amounts of information, or to work with machines that do.

Learning Our Roles: Literature as Software

If the brain's prefrontal lobes are the hard wiring that nature provides, then society, as it has for many centuries, provides the software programming, in the form of stories and literature. Myths and legends, stories and tales are how we prime our younger generation to take up the roles of adulthood. The earliest stories refer to the simplest roles and qualities—good and bad, wise and foolish, male and female. And while stories have been with us from before recorded history, it is most interesting to note that the modern corpus of fairy tales has probably been around for fewer than a thousand years.

I would suggest that society took an evolutionary leap when we moved from simple agrarian roles to more complex urban ones. Urbanization provides the opportunity, and in fact the demand, to function with multiple and simultaneous roles. Fairy tales and stories become more complex as the need to function in these different roles increases. It is not coincidence that the time required for education has expanded greatly in the past thousand years. We are now at a point where the most complex professions require almost half of one's life in order to prepare to practice them. It is certain that, as we go forward, *Homo neticus* will be a constantly learning, auto-evolving creature.

So what is the literature that *Homo neticus* will evolve in order to create the programming necessary for our children?[1] The concept here is *literature as software* for the roles that society expects us to adopt. Through literature, we get to explore both the inner workings and outer manifestations of dozens, indeed hundreds, of roles in a safe, fictional way.

I suggest that this is one of the primary functions of literature in any society. Literature is the play that the adult mind requires, in the same way that young children require play to process their earliest inputs. Literature enables adult minds to take up and examine interesting roles that they may or may not ever assume in real life. One might argue that fantasy and science fiction have become increasingly important genres of fiction because they so consistently push the limits of imaginable roles. Even the horror genre may fall into this category, as life imitates art in the grotesque revelations of our daily newspapers.

The Future

We raised the question of *Homo sapiens* evolving into *Homo neticus*, but that still leaves us with the question of the coevolution of *Homo neticus* and the fourth kingdom. So what's in store? What does the future hold for the fourth kingdom as it relates to humanity?

As fourth kingdom organisms increasingly dominate the world, the social landscape will necessarily change. Corporations may well become sentient, and they may no longer be content to remain subordinate to their fourth kingdom cousins, the countries. If corporations are alive in this sense, then by definition they will

---

[1] Literature is considered in its broadest sense to include every possible genre: movies, plays, books, and so on, as well as fairy tales and urban legends.

evolve. What are some of the evolutionary developments that we can anticipate as a result? One speculation is that, since countries have stalled in their thrust to explore space, corporations will take up the slack, thanks in part to the drive to accumulate capital.

I have speculated elsewhere about the creation of a space university, which I envisioned as a transformational organization that will facilitate and encourage space exploration.[2] There is little doubt in my mind that denizens of the fourth kingdom, in one form or another, will bring us into space. In fact, I predict that leaving the planet and exploring the solar system and the galaxy beyond will be among the primary tasks of fourth kingdom organisms in the years to come.

An aside: one thing to which we have alluded, but spoken relatively little about, is the interrelationships among companies, and the nature of the ecosystems that businesses create. Industries become like species in such an analysis, and markets are comparable to community ecosystems. The effects of globalization force large-cap companies to compete and diversify in a single worldwide financial ecosystem. We are tempted to call this the financial ecosystem, or "fin-ecosystem," and I see it as a distinguishing feature of our business future.

Here we revisit the other denizens of the fourth kingdom, especially countries, to show how they participate in the fin-ecosystem. Markets are viewed as means to generate, harvest, and recycle the capital that fourth kingdom creatures need, the way plants and animals rely on the manufacture of simple sugars. Equity, bond, and foreign exchange markets are high-level intercommunity networks that enable these systems to trade resources and make

---

[2] See my article "Academy of Space Studies: Planning for a Spacefaring Future" (Sirkin, 1991).

available the information capital that is locked up in them. Global markets evolve, as does all other life, toward the more efficient use of resources.

The Cycle Continues

The emergence of new sentient species—those that inhabit the fourth kingdom—is enabling many dramatic things to happen: the birth of a true global economy, the emergence of a truly interconnected communication network, and the desire to take these newfound abilities beyond the earth's surface.

Will it be clear cosmic sailing? Of course not. Luddites emerge in every generation. We will hear talk of conflict—individualism versus corporatism, and certainly countries versus corporations— as the fourth kingdom becomes an arena for conflict. We have already seen intimations of this in the previous century, in the form of multinationals versus governments. Such dynamic tensions are good and necessary manifestations of the dynamic equilibrium that is characteristic of the natural world. Species come and species go. Some are better adapted to one landscape, while others are better suited to a future one, and this is as it should be.

Naturalists such as E. O. Wilson (1999) may bemoan the end of diversity, but as we go forward, I am among those celebrating the creation of new life and the emergence of new species where none existed before.[3]

---

[3] Wilson argues that the frightening rate of extinction is unparalleled and dangerous. While I am no advocate of ecological irresponsibility, it must also be acknowledged that species become extinct constantly, and this is part of the ebb and flow of life on the planet. New species arise to take their place.

Upon rereading this chapter for the second edition, I am struck by how true some of the predictions here have been demonstrated to be, and the sheer unpredictability of scientific and business research. The internet and Moore's Law have combined to create a world barely imaginable when this chapter was first written: talking household appliances, self-driving cars, and huge strides in AI and IOT are transforming the world. Private companies have indeed begun exploring space, and some are predicting that soon AI-powered corporations will not even need people to function, make money, or control their environment.

11

PEOPLE WHO NEED PEOPLE: UNDERSTANDING AND DEVELOPING HUMAN CAPITAL, THE ULTIMATE RESOURCE

Introduction to Human Capital: Scientific and Historical Perspectives

*H*uman capital—it's an ABSTRACt way of talking about the people in an organization, what they know, their intelligence, their competence, and their talent. It refers to what people in a company know that allows them to address a need, fix a problem, or otherwise translate their human capabilities into financial capital. Human capital is the means by which people turn their knowledge into wealth for the benefit of themselves and the organization that employs them.

The concept of human capital goes well beyond the corporate quest for profit. I believe there is a biological imperative, as deeply rooted as our tendency to act socially, which enables and encourages us to behave in ways that lead to the creation of human capital. This human capital imperative, as it may be called, is evolutionarily new and extremely powerful. It influences our cultures, gives modern societies their character, and has enabled us to reach levels of comfort and productivity hardly imagined a mere hundred years ago.

People are not machines that are built for a single purpose, used until they run down, and then replaced. People must be developed, nurtured, coaxed, managed, educated, strengthened, and skill-enabled. To be of use, their knowledge must be codified into processes and applied strategically toward a greater goal.

This is the genius of the modern organization—to transform the human capabilities of its workers into productive efforts that result in financial capital accruing to the individual and the company.

The term "human capital" sounds abstract, perhaps even dehumanizing. Yet it is the most human thing in the world. Freud told us that love and work are the pillars upon which fulfilling lives are built. Work is not simply activity, and it is not random. For work to be fulfilling, it must be valuable, i.e., appreciated and ultimately paid for in some manner. How is it that some human activities generate value beyond the moment in time in which they occur? How does human capital, the know-how employed by workers to get the job done, translate into financial capital, or profit? What are the opportunities for improving human capital, for individuals as well as for the company as a whole, to maximize the human potential of an organization and return higher profits?

Business Capital, Human and Otherwise: Some Definitions

If intellectual capital comprises the intangible assets of a company, then human capital is that part of those assets that goes home every night with the employees. Human capital is the know-how inside employees' heads that allows them to use the other assets of the company to earn a profit. Let's looks at the different forms of intellectual capital that a company may possess, as well as its tangible assets.

Hard assets

Hard assets are the stuff accountants love because they can touch, count, and most importantly depreciate those assets. These are the plants, tools, computers, and machines that ran the old economy.

Financial reserves can also be hard assets: money in the bank, stocks, warrants, and investments in other companies, among other instruments. Again, these things are calculable and there tends to be agreement as to how to determine their value.

The *balance sheet*, which is comprised of various ratios relating hard assets to income, is a general statement of a company's value. The problem with hard assets is that the very thing that makes them easy to calculate—the fact that their costs are known because the money for them has been spent—makes them unhelpful in calculating future value. Build a plant, staff it, stock it, and you know what that costs. This is the realm of traditional accounting. When we want to know how to extract additional value from these same assets through enhancing processes or developing people, we have entered the world of intangible assets.

Process Capital

Process capital comprises the methods, techniques, and know-how that a company employs to create a product or deliver a service. It refers to the company's unique and evolved structure that enables it to do whatever it does to earn revenue. Process capital is often but not always at the heart of a company's success.

If the company is a manufacturing facility, process capital may be the exact way in which it makes, sells, and delivers widgets. The company may have unique capabilities in any of these areas that give it some special advantage. At the very least, it has enough capability in one or more of these areas to enable it to be profitable. If not, it could not survive.

Customer Capital

Some companies have a unique relationship with their customers. The company is trusted to provide a service or make a product that customers value so highly that they are loyal beyond price, service, or availability. Fans, for example, are a form of customer capital that give value to media properties.

Of course, no product is totally immune to market forces, but products and companies with high customer capital are often forgiven for a multitude of sins. This investment of value into a product over and above its "real" value represents the customer capital—sometimes referred to as brand capital. Accountants have tried to put a value on this good will, but customer capital is difficult to measure.

Human Capital

Human capital is none of the above. It pertains to what people know that enables them to come together to make a company successful. While it would be inaccurate to say that human capital is more important than hard assets, process capital, or customer capital, we can say that without human capital, nothing else would be worth much for long.

In other words, the absence of human capital will sink a company faster than the absence of any other kind of capital. Furthermore, human capital enables the leverage of all of the other types of capital. Without it, there is no company; with it, there is always a chance of success.

Lagging Indicators v. Leading Indicators

A large segment of the financial industry is charged with determining what a company is worth. Traditional accounting methods have relied on lagging indicators to determine a company's book value. *Book value* is simply the hard assets minus the hard liabilities. If one were to break up the company, sell its assets, and pay its bills, then the book value is what would be left. Valuation of hard assets corresponds to a valuation of lagging indicators. The problem is that they both look at the company through a rearview mirror.

There is another way to determine what a company is worth. Take its current stock price, multiply that by the number shares, and we have a value based on what investors are willing to pay for a company, or at least its parts. This is called *market value*. It's an interesting number because factored into it are the expectations of how a company will leverage its tangible assets with its intangible assets to be successful in the future. The difference between book value and market value is an indirect measure of the value of a company's intangible assets.

Much of the variance in a stock's price is attributed to the fate of the industry the company is in, when all other things are equal. That is, if Company X in the consumer products industry is experiencing a falling stock price, it's quite likely that *all* consumer products companies are experiencing similar falls, due to their common financial environment. But within an industry, the difference between one company's prospects and another's is often attributable to the intangibles: brand, know-how, leadership.

In today's highly competitive and forward-looking environment, intangible assets determine the true valuation of a company. And the enabler of intangible assets is human capital. Without human capital, a corporation is like a giant, state-of-the-art rocket ship: powered by the most advanced technology, capable of flying on autopilot for a while, but not autonomous. The crew, its human capital, knows where it is going and can provide midcourse corrections, and emergency response. The crew can even change course when the need arises.

Why Human Capital, and Why Now

Human capital is not a new term; it has been around for at least twenty-five years. There has been quite a bit of recent interest in human capital, from the *HR Scorecard* (Becker, Huselid, & Ulrich, 1999) to *The ROI of Human Capital* (Fitz-enz, 2000).

These books offer valuable insights, especially for the CEO or human resources executive who must justify and measure expenditures on human capital. Yet an understanding of human capital is even more important from other perspectives.

Human capital for individuals

Career management is about handling your own human capital. Just as a growing number of individual investors have taken increasing responsibility for investing their own retirement portfolios, more and more people are taking responsibility for the development of their human capital.

The parallels are striking. In a bygone era, professional money managers handled the investments of most people who had the disposable income to invest. While money managers are not extinct, demand for their services has declined. Similarly, human capital was once managed by others in a corporate environment. It was left to the HR professionals and senior management to decide whom to develop, what to develop, how far, and how fast.

Times have changed, and they continue to change at an accelerated pace. Skill sets and competencies of today will evolve, and some will become extinct. New skills, which will follow on innovation as night follows day, will be required and marketable in the future.

The very nature of work and people's relationship to it are changing. For example, Daniel Pink (1998), in his book *Free Agent Nation*, has suggested that future models of work will be based less on the current *Fortune 500* and more on the entertainment production industry. The idea is that there are sets of skills required for a particular project. Professionals with the requisite skill set will get hired to do a project, in the same way that scores of professionals come together to produce a movie. They will be contracted with and paid according to their ability to provide a specific service. Their value, and therefore their fees, will be determined based on a combination of their overall contribution and the going rate for that kind of service in the marketplace. There will be little expectation to continue on in that particular project because it will have a beginning and an end. The best workers can hope for is to perform quality work that speaks for itself so they will be in demand among future producers of that kind of work. In addition to payment, the worker's goal for working on a project will be to enhance the constellation of skills that makes them employable and able to command good rates. Although this may seem like a step back from the security of the past, some will find it a welcome development that ensures opportunities and rewards based on contribution, not on position.

Regardless of whether we approve of these changes, they are coming. Some, like Pink, argue that they are already here. Your human capital portfolio, which lists skills and competencies that you possess, is your key to future employment. As with any other important tools, your best interest lies in knowing what they are, keeping them sharp, and being on the lookout for new and useful ones.

For the second edition, it is relevant to point out that, in part through the ubiquity of the internet and other technologies, Pink's free-agent nation has arrived and is currently called "the gig economy." While not all jobs are part-time or temporary, many more are now than when this, or Pink's book, was originally written. The trend seems set to continue apace.

Human capital for leaders and managers

Individual human capital, while necessary, is not sufficient for an organization to succeed in the marketplace. Organizational leaders must know how to leverage individual competencies into organizational competencies. I will refer to this as group human capital (GHC).

GHC is the skill set of specialized groups within the company that allow it to make, sell, or deliver its products or services. These competencies can be ordered along a continuum from core, and therefore essential, to peripheral, and potentially outsourceable. To identify the GHC for a particular company is to understand what its people, as they come together to work, do best. It is a way of determining how a company should be making its profit and how a company *could* be making its profit.

Leaders must a have global, strategic view of GHC that is unique to their company. Managers must have a specific, tactical view of these same competencies. Understanding how individual human capital comes together to create group human capital is the essence of building teams.

Human capital for investors and analysts

Valuing a company is no easy task. There is no universal agreement about how to assess the relevant variables. Market uncertainty, stock price fluctuations, and competing estimates of earnings are all indications of the many unknowns that must be factored in. As the economy evolves from an industrial base to an information base, the amount of value attributable to knowledge and know-how will increase proportionately. Some of this value is captured in the processes and techniques that I have referred to as process capital. But for all the process capital, there must exist human capital to give those processes life.

Imagine an assembly line. It contains the machines that facilitate the assembly of raw materials. It is structured according to a methodology that is based on experience, customer needs, optimum workflows, and dozens of other variables. People add value to this process when they contribute their know-how, when they solve unexpected problems, and when they make changes that add value in innovative ways. People bring human capital to the process, and this, more than any other factor, will account for sustained business success over time.

Analysts are increasingly required to estimate not simply what a company is worth now (via its lagging indicators) but what it will be worth in the future. Stock price has evolved from being based primarily on lagging indicators to forward indicators. These forward indicators rely heavily on evaluating corporate assets that will add value in the future. Among the most certain of such assets are the human capital assets.

In order to understand and effectively use these insights, we must develop a better way to inventory, develop, and account for human capital. Ultimately the value of the company is at stake.

12

WONDERFUL BUSINESS: ORGANIZATIONAL EVOLUTION IN THE FOURTH KINGDOM

I f we were to create a taxonomy of the fourth kingdom, it would be a challenging task indeed. I've discussed elsewhere in this book how the list of phyla within the fourth kingdom might include religions, states, and universities. Of course, our focus is on business organizations. If fourth kingdom phyla, and particularly businesses, are indeed living things, then we expect them to conform to, or at least parallel, some of the evolutionary phenomena we've seen in other natural life on the planet.

Although Charles Darwin thought that evolution was a slowly progressing and rather linear affair, Stephen Jay Gould and Niles Eldredge have suggested an alternative idea: the theory of punctuated equilibrium. They posit and demonstrate, with a mountain of convincing evidence, that evolution proceeds in fits and starts. Periods of wild growth are often preceded by mass extinctions and then followed by long periods of stability. For example, life on our planet was fairly stable for at least a billion years, and then came the great Cambrian explosion, with scores of new body designs and hundreds of phyla of multicellular creatures emerging that were never seen before (and indeed have not been seen since). Another example of this pattern is the great Permian extinction, which preceded the rise of the dinosaurs.

With these facts of natural history in mind, let's take a quick look back at the evolution of companies and corporations as we know them today.

In the Beginning

Many might say that corporate organizations began with medieval guilds. In our definition, however, a corporate organization must be profit-making, and medieval guilds were initially formed simply to protect the interests of their members. They were probably more like trade unions than corporations.

The very first corporate organizations, rather, were most likely monasteries and convents. These organizations were owned by the various orders of the Catholic Church, and existed across Europe for multiple generations. While they certainly did not set out to make a profit, it is no secret that many of them acquired great wealth over the centuries, and became powerful within the Catholic Church and beyond. It's safe to say that they are among the oldest extant organizations of any kind.

The Catholic Church itself, of course, represents an organization in the same phylum as monasteries and convents that has existed for centuries in close to its current form. As for other phyla, we can point to universities, many of which have existed for hundreds of years, as related types of fourth kingdom organisms.

Today, three distinct features characterize modern corporations. They have more than one member (the relatively recent S corporations and LLCs being potential exceptions), they have assets that are distinguishable from the private assets of their members, and they have a formal system of management or hierarchy of control. As such, they are a fairly recent legal invention.

We can trace the origin of the corporation to the very first organized efforts to explore and trade. Available historical records indicate that even groups of Athenian and Phoenician merchants were sometimes willing to pool their funds, build trading vessels, and organize ventures. But we distinguish these from corporate organizations because they were essentially *partnerships*. The modern corporation, rather, is founded on the distribution of risk and the ability of its members to remain anonymous if they so choose—hence the French corporation abbreviation "SA," for *société anonyme*.

The earliest modern companies were actually joint ventures between political states and groups of businessmen. Often the companies were conceived of as arms of the government rather than as true commercial ventures. An example of an early company is the British East India Company, chartered by Queen Elizabeth, the Earl of Cumberland, and others to trade East Indies goods and generally oversee the lands that Great Britain occupied. The Royal African Company and the Hudson Bay Company were similarly chartered. We can probably state with accuracy that the New World was explored and settled primarily due to these early corporate entities pursuing their quest for capital.

In the nineteenth century, common law formally recognized the corporation as an entity with rights and obligations, introducing the concept of the modern business. The modern corporation is today less than 150 years old, and is therefore really in its evolutionary infancy. Nevertheless, if evolutionary parallels hold, we can expect the evolution of this fourth kingdom phylum to demonstrate periods of rapid growth, followed by stability. Indeed, we have seen precisely this in recent decades.

Events Give Rise to New Life Forms

Economic opportunities do indeed give rise to flurries of business activity. The advent of railroads over 150 years ago in the United States created a stock-market bubble and a race to found as many railway companies as possible. In turn, this was followed by a crash and consolidation, which ultimately enabled railways to crisscross the North American continent.

With the advent of the small combustible engine in the late nineteenth century, a number of small-engine manufacturers rushed into the automobile business. Many of the Big Three's popular brands began as separate companies in the early part of the twentieth century. It is not a coincidence that the crash of 1929 occurred simultaneously with the realization that there weren't enough people or roads to sustain all this transportation activity.

These are sequences of historical events that Stephen Jay Gould, and perhaps even Darwin himself, might acknowledge as having evolutionary predictability. The industries in question saw a rush of attempts to exploit a new technology, followed by a contraction based on marketplace realities, to be followed by sustained growth in a more stable business environment.

In recent years, the dot-com boom and bust represent another retelling of the same tale. It should surprise no one that the boom of the Internet years, which was larger and stronger than the earlier innovation explosions mentioned above, should be followed by an economic contraction of similar scale. The great, sustainable innovations based on Internet technology have yet to be realized, but natural history tells us they are inevitable.

What a difference 15 years make! Indeed, while and soon after the first edition of this book was written, companies such as Google, Facebook, and Amazon became business behemoths following this precise trajectory.

Wonderful Business

There are more lessons to be gleaned from the early Cambrian era. Most fascinating to the biodynamically informed observer are the parallels between business in the 1990s and the Cambrian explosion of prehistory.[1]

In the pre-Cambrian era, we had a world occupied almost exclusively by single-celled or small multicellular creatures. There was a tremendous opportunity for larger multicellular organisms to evolve in these relatively unpopulated waters—unpopulated in terms of *levels* of life, if not numbers of life forms. That is, we have no reason to believe there were not large numbers of organisms, but there were not large numbers of ecological niches filled by many different types of organisms. It was the populating of levels and niches that comprised the Cambrian explosion.

The planet experimented during this period with life forms that were interesting and, for lack of a better word, creative—yet highly unstable. Does this language not precisely describe the dot-com business environment in the 1990s? I think it does. A large number of new organizational types emerged during that decade, many of which have since fallen by the wayside. Yet the sheer excitement of that level of activity will be long remembered by those who participated in this Cambrian explosion of global business forms.

---

[1] For readers interested in the Cambrian explosion, I highly recommend Stephen Jay Gould's (1989) classic *Wonderful Life*, from which the title of this chapter was adapted.

Venture funds, in the case of the dot-com era, demonstrate these phenomena. Venture capitalists, and the business incubators and "business accelerators" they established, provided the natural surroundings that nurtured new Internet-age growth. The marketplace was able to support venture funds, which seeded many early-stage companies. Again, it should be no surprise that most of these ventures failed, as that is the regular fate of new experiments of nature. Survival of the fittest? Let's be less absolute and simply state that the strong tend to survive, in business as in nature.

Other business organisms that thrived during this time included *rollups* (the amalgamation of small businesses into large ones), spin-offs, spinouts, and mergers and acquisitions of all sizes and stripes. Related business life forms that we would expect to see in more mature markets—outsourcing organizations and the like—did not thrive, because they require a more stable business ecosystem in which to exist.

The reader will recall the differentiation principle from the axioms discussed in Part I of this book—the idea that systems tend to become increasingly complex, to differentiate their parts, over time. This has certainly happened in the evolution of the corporation phylum under discussion here, as not only have corporate structures become more complex, but so have the legal underpinnings required to support them. (The state of Delaware, in its legal devotion to enabling the increasingly complex structure of U.S. corporations, is itself worthy of a chapter. And Nevada is rapidly evolving its own competitive position in this regard.)

Coevolution, the Environment, and the Inevitable Increase of Complexity

One of evolution's most compelling lessons is that only in the context of an environment, and of sustainability within that environment, can life forms develop the qualities they need to survive. This is what modern evolutionary biologists mean when they speak about a *fitness landscape*.

Coevolution refers to a process within an ecosystem through which creatures, by their very existence, enhance the opportunities for other creatures. It is a characteristic of successful ecosystems to have many such relationships. Bees and flowers are the classic example—flowers could not survive without the bees to pollinate them, and bees could not survive without the pollen of flowers.[2]

Increasing levels of complexity are part of the coevolutionary equation. There are no more complex creatures on the planet than the denizens of the fourth kingdom. Let's look briefly at a company poised to take advantage of the sustainable innovations based on Internet technology that have yet to be realized.

That company is Executive Development Corporation (EDC). (As noted in a previous chapter, as of the second edition of this book, EDC has morphed and been acquired multiple times. It no longer has an independent existence.) As a cofounder and director of this company, I had an intimate involvement with its founding and growth. We began EDC with a typical corporate inventory: assets, stock, and a business model. It was a plain-vanilla Delaware C corporation.

---

[2] Another highly interesting discussion of coevolutionary phenomena between plants and humans can be found in Michael Pollan's 2001 book *The Botany of Desire*.

Among several corporate forms we considered, but did not pursue, was one that was particularly interesting. In order to fairly distribute responsibility and income, we considered forming a separate organization—let's call it Leadership LLC—that would then have been hired by EDC to run that organization. An LLC is a limited liability corporation, which is a relatively new organizational form that protects its members from liability beyond that of the C corporation. In this example, the LLC would have taken as its compensation a percentage of profits, leaving EDC intact as a largely traditional corporation.

This is similar to the phenomenon biologists speculate happened billions of years ago, when a small prokaryotic (single-cell, unnucleated) organism "agreed" to become the nucleus for another prokaryotic organism, thereby giving rise to the first eukaryotic (single-celled, nucleated) organisms—a process known as *symbiogenesis*. The entire chain of evolution beyond bacteria-like organisms that followed hinged on this accomplishment.

It is interesting to note that an earlier organizational form, the LLP, or limited liability partnership, is even more complex. In this organizational form, there are two groups of partners: a group of limited liability partners and a general partner. The general partner can be yet another corporation created expressly for this purpose. The limited liability partners are protected from most of the liability that the LLP shoulders. The general partner is liable. When the general partner is a corporate entity, it provides additional insulation to its members.

In this form, which is the traditional organizational form of many law firms, we see a similar instance of an organization (the LLP) controlled by another organization (the corporate general partner), which is constructed to shield its members from additional liability. It is a complex, hierarchically nested organization.

Although I am not a legal expert in corporate forms, it seems safe to conclude that even more complex organizational forms exist now and will continue to be invented during the current time period, the business world's own Cambrian explosion.

Dominating an Ecosystem—Natural or Commercial

The history of evolution seems to indicate that acts of coming together tend to be more common and lasting than split-offs. This is probably because once organisms come together and cooperate in a symbiotic fashion, they quickly eliminate functions and structures that they previously needed but no longer do. Their ability to survive on their own, in other words, goes away.

But is this true on a corporate level? I suggest that it is, and that a good example of this is Microsoft Corporation. Microsoft has a history of joining with smaller companies in order to market products in partnership. It then either incorporates this product into its own product line, as it did with Excel and PowerPoint, or it chooses to disable key features of those products and let them die off. Whether this represents an example of predatory business practice or a series of incremental business decisions is a subject for other business theorists, or perhaps the U.S. legal system, to ponder. These practices have made some businesses and entrepreneurs wealthy, while others have met an ignominious demise. The point is that once a product adjusts to the Microsoft environment, it is no longer viable on its own. As of the printing of the second edition, we continue to see examples of this phenomenon. For example, in the cell phone industry, we often hear talk of phone ecosystems, including applications (apps), hardware, and software innovations that work for one company's phones but not others, e.g., Apple versus Samsung.

As with their soft-bodied analogues, when corporate organizations go about exploiting their systemic niches, *scale* matters. The strategies that companies use to exploit their market niches impact greatly on their size, and vice versa. It is difficult for a 10-person organization to be a global entity, just as it is hard for a 100,000-person organization not to have a significant impact on numerous other businesses. Let's examine this issue from biggest to smallest.

Location, Location, Location

Large global organizations—say the *Fortune 100*, or organizations of over 50,000 people—are similar to what ecologists call *lead species or keystone species* within ecosystems. The lead species is the species around which many or most of the species in that ecosystem regulate their activity. The lead species is usually not at the top of the food chain, nor is it at the bottom. Rather, the members of lead species tend simply to dominate an area due to great numbers, or to shape their environment in particularly significant and impactful ways.

A lead species in a business dominates that business ecosystem, and other businesses grow up around it. A large company that exists in a city in which few other large companies have been established is clearly the economic driver in that city. The number of jobs that it affects directly is significant enough, but the number of businesses and amount of economic activity in its orbit is often three to five times greater than that. In the environs of a large plant or office building, there are countless auxiliary services, from the food-service entrepreneur who parks his sandwich truck outside the front door to the search professionals who help staff the company's executive suite. The largest businesses can sustain hundreds, if not thousands, of these auxiliary businesses, just as a particular species in a natural ecosystem can be the linchpin of the fate of scores of other species.

In business, a dominant organization in a particular industry, especially a new one in an undeveloped region, can attract others. This impacts the geographical region as well. Places become known as the "natural" homes to specific industries. This is because the auxiliary organizations that arise to support one large business make the location an attractive place for others in the industry to settle. Detroit has become a synecdoche for the auto industry. The Ford Corporation's birthplace became the home for an entire global industry. Hollywood, because of the need for good light and little rain, became the magnet for one production company, then several, and then an entire movie industry. Examples abound throughout the history of business, from the industries and city-states created by the regular flooding of the Nile to Swiss banks to Nashville's country music industry.

On Being Too Big and Too Rich—The Things You Don't Learn in Business School

A lead species has to be of a certain size in order to sustain all the organizations in its orbit and create a self-sustaining dynamic equilibrium. Big doesn't necessarily survive better than small. Rather, as E. O. Wilson has argued, in his books on the subject of biological diversity, the health of an ecosystem directly correlates with the number of diverse species it supports and can continue to maintain. The ecosystems at risk are those with only a few major players.

Once again, the same holds true for business and industry: Diversity and differentiation are far more important than size. Markets become inherently unhealthy when the ecosystem that is the industry fails to offer a vibrant mix of companies of various sizes and a wide breadth of product and service offerings. Businesses evolve with the dueling agendas of growing ever larger and finding additional market niches to exploit. There probably exists an optimal size for most businesses. A business can become too big and unsustainable, too "fat and sloppy." The now-defunct behemoth AOL Time Warner became such a megaplayer that it lost its lead in every market in which it operated.

One theory about the extinction of dinosaurs is that they simply grew too large to be viable. They had to eat constantly to sustain a bulk that was often too unwieldy and costly (in calories) to maintain. Indeed, the word "dinosaur," often used in a business context, has come to mean something too big and old to sustain itself.

Clayton Christiansen (1997), in *The Innovator's Dilemma*, has pointed out that such growth isn't merely a dilemma in terms of resources, it's a dilemma in terms of function as well. Corporate organisms, he demonstrated, arrive at a financial equilibrium that balances size, form, and function, and creates a sustainable business model. For the largest of companies, sustainable business models require huge amounts of both input and output. These companies—again, think of the example of AOL Time Warner—spend tremendous amounts of money and make tremendous amounts of money. Yet their very success is what dooms them. Like the giant anteater that's an expert at finding and eating ants, when the market conditions change—or the anthills wash away in a heavy rain—these unwieldy, specialized creatures find themselves adrift in an environment for which they are no longer fit.

Scaling down a bit, middle-tier companies represent the bulk of businesses in the world today. If one thinks of larger companies as lead species, then these middle-size companies constitute all the other companies in their orbit. Smaller companies have certain advantages that make them highly sustainable and, in many ways, more robust than their larger counterparts. Less dependent on a constant input of fuel (i.e., capital), more maneuverable, more responsive to the market, and faster on the uptake, they are like the omnivores in an ecosystem—those small mammals, like skunks and raccoons, that will leave no stone unturned and no opportunity unexploited in their search for a meal.

From Meals to Deals

Midsize companies are not more successful. Success is dependent on diversity, and neither big nor small equates to health or robustness. Darwin taught that survival is ultimately the only meaningful test of success. But smaller businesses create market efficiencies in places where larger businesses have needs, but cannot always exploit them.

When I was consulting to the now-defunct Lucent Technologies, in that company's heyday, executives regularly refused business opportunities with yields of less than a billion dollars a year. Anything less than that was simply not worth the time and effort. However, this fact created innumerable opportunities for companies and executives who were more than happy to participate in deals at the sub-billion dollar level. In fact, many new businesses are created in just this manner. Scavenging, as it were, plays a huge role in both natural and business ecosystems— it's what makes the system efficient.

If you're a giant *Tyrannosaurus rex* who needs five carcasses a day just to keep going, you're not going to stoop to pick up the scraps that fall by your feet. However, there may be a whole ecosystem of small carnivores that can survive quite nicely on your leavings. As on the African veldt, lead carnivores take down prey, and the buzzards and hyenas clean it up. Or think of the dung beetle that lives off the leavings of elephants.

The same holds true with large organizations. They simply don't have the efficiencies of scale to exploit every opportunity, but that fact leaves some opportunities for smaller, nimbler, and hungrier followers. This is the world of the midsize business.

And what about small companies? Small companies may be comparable to the insects and microorganisms within a large ecosystem. Small businesses are usually local, have a minimum number of employees, and are quite often family owned. These are businesses run by local entrepreneurs who see an opportunity and make the best of it. Of course, small businesses can grow into medium-size businesses, and medium-size businesses can grow to large businesses, but I would argue that each category is distinct.

The Human Factor

It may seem that the analogies I draw between corporations and natural systems serve only to reduce complex human interactions to mere "animal" status. They may appear to imply that we are like mindless ants or bees in a hive. I am, in fact, saying no such thing.

In nature, biology truly is destiny, but in business, *free will* means that the corporate morphology is far more plastic than that of natural systems.

Because of their *human* elements, business entities can change and evolve based on the needs and creativity of the people who constitute them. Flexibility and exchange do happen within the phyla of the fourth kingdom—hence the next chapter on the kingdom's human, emotional face.

13

"BEHOLD HOMO NETICUS"

The Human Face of the Fourth Kingdom

In the preceding essay, I promised to touch on the fourth kingdom's human, emotional face. So before plunging into the concept of *Homo neticus*, let me do just that—diverge briefly into the nature of *emotions* in relation to our humanity.

Charles Darwin wrote some of the earliest essays about human emotion from an evolutionary point of view. Psychoanalytic psychology, while giving a prominent place to affect, proceeded to reduce all affect to an expression of sexual instincts. I have stated elsewhere (Sirkin and Fleming, 1985) that Freud, in his concern for finding the root energy of the human personality, was on the right track. I think his exclusive focus on sexuality, however, is needlessly limiting. The emotions themselves are necessary and sufficient primary drivers for the human personality. The added reductionism to the sexual instincts is both misguided and unnecessary.

In the past century, behaviorists reduced emotion, along with every other important psychological construct, to a set of behaviors. This represented a hopelessly simplistic treatment of the rich inner life of emotions, and an unnecessary procrustean bed upon which to delimit the study of human being. The "cognitivization" of psychology and the study of emotions has the potential to admit both behavior and inner manifestations of emotional phenomena. The jury is still out as to whether psychology can do justice to Darwin's original, elegant treatment over one hundred and fifty years ago.

Scientists have demonstrated that humans experience at least six or seven basic emotions, among them *joy, interest, surprise, anger, fear, sadness,* and *disgust* (see Izard, 1977; Ekman, 2003). (See Figure 13-1.) The fact that most five-year-olds can read emotional cues in the simplest of line drawings is quite compelling, as are the other developmental and cross-cultural data in this field.

I am among a small group of psychologists who believe that emotions are the primary motivational system of human beings, and that such emotions are in fact hard-wired into our bodies and psyches.

One can only wonder at the warped view of mankind that led some psychologists in past decades to emphasize cognition at the expense of emotion. It seems clear that we are in fact nothing if not bundles of emotions wrapped in a veneer of cognition. If the prefrontal cortex of the brain represents much of our cognitive ability, then a good portion of our more primitive functions are dedicated to emotions.

Any discussion of being human must address the question, "What is the role of emotions?"[1] Many religious philosophies, such as Buddhism and even traditional Christian practices, emphasize the mastery of emotion as the road to enlightenment. In seeming contradiction, almost every religion has a contrasting mystical aspect that encourages an emotional path toward enlightenment. Whether emotions are to be mastered or embraced, they are an inextricable aspect of our humanness.

Because they are so integral, emotions necessarily play an important part in our roles as participants in fourth kingdom enterprises. In other words, emotions, directed through the roles people adopt, drive or energize our interactions with others as we give life to fourth kingdom meaning communities. Emotions are the drivers of human interaction at higher levels.

The Renaissance Redux

The Latin exhortation "*ecce homo*" (pronounced e-chā-ˈhō-mō)—behold the man—for some has Christian connotations. For me, it epitomizes the values of the Renaissance. Hearing the phrase always makes me think of Leonardo da Vinci's famous anatomical sketch, often framed by the immortal phrase, "Man is the measure of all things." There was a time when humanity was able to find its place in the universe by using Galileo's telescopic inquiries or the works of artists and literati, all of whom helped to expand a growing sense of man's place in the world.

---

[1] For the sake of discussion, we will use the generic term "emotions" to represent the subjective feelings as well as the behavioral manifestation of emotional expression. The fact that some emotions are felt but not expressed, while others are unfelt but nevertheless operative (as in cases of denial) should not deter a more general discussion of these phenomena.

In contemporary times, however, people have described an "information Renaissance" sweeping the globe. Talk of the industrial economy has yielded to talk of the information economy, and communication technology has changed humanity's sense of self. We have entered a new stage of evolution—a stage at which individuals are networked with other individuals so that a true global consciousness has emerged.

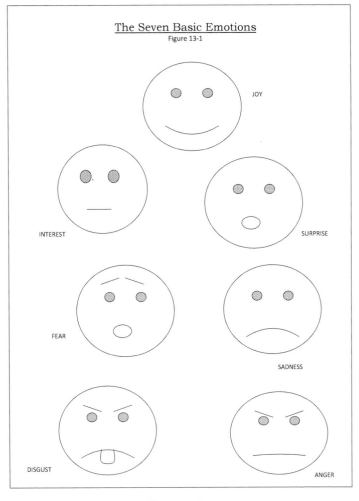

Figure 13-1

The French philosopher Pierre Teilhard de Chardin (1965) spoke of it in his concept of the *noosphere*, an overarching planetary consciousness that exists above any individual or group of individuals.

More recently, the *Gaia hypothesis*—put forth by British chemist James Lovelock (1988) and the American biologist Lynn Margulis—conceived of the earth's living matter (including air, oceans, and land surface) as a complex single system that can be viewed as one organism.

While these ideas—the *noosphere* and the *Gaia* hypothesis—are consistent with biodynamic theory, and in some ways may be seen as its precursors, there are new phenomena that force us to amend some of these earlier ideas. Specifically, the coevolution of information and technology has led to the ubiquitousness of communication devices that have in themselves created, in biofeedback terms, a *feed-forward loop*—engendering even more communication devices.

If, up to this point, we have been known collectively as *Homo sapiens* ("man the wise"), we might refer to this more modern version as *Homo communicans* ("man the communicator"). Even more profound, however, is the emergence of *Homo neticus*—"man the networked."

Remember that coevolution is a phenomenon that occurs when two species affect each other's evolution such that the evolutionary qualities of one species develop to take advantage of the evolutionary qualities of the other, to the mutual benefit of both. I believe that humanity has entered into a coevolutionary relationship with its own artifacts. While man is not the only tool-using animal in the world, it seems clear that man is the only tool-using animal that has entered into a relationship with those tools such that they are coevolving together.

While we can talk about technology for food production and technology for habitation or housing, nowhere has the coevolutionary process been more salient than in information technology. In this vein, one could say that man has been evolving information technology since the earliest days of writing, and possibly well before—perhaps even since the earliest days of speech.

The earliest writing was an information technology that allowed for the development of complex societies. In all probability, it was simply a form of record keeping that allowed Sumerians to track the inputs and outputs of their storehouses, and thereby provide the information backbone to the first great known civilization.

The next step in this historical communication-evolution juggernaut would have been books, beginning with the collection of wisdom in the form of scrolls or folios. We begin to enter modern historical consciousness when we consider how the book has changed our sense of ourselves. From the people of the book to the written literature of entire peoples, we have seen the reification—the making manifest—of a culture or a people's history in the form of text. This monumental event created profound changes in our understanding of ourselves.

With the advent of the printing press, the wisdom of books was suddenly available to everyone, and progress accelerated. The industrial revolution was ushered in only a few hundred years later.

Each of these innovations represented a stepwise or logarithmic increase in humanity's ability to process, share, and develop information. Each innovation enabled even more innovation at an ever-faster pace.

I believe, however, that all of these past innovations will pale in comparison to the amount of information-sharing enabled by current and future man-machine interactivity.

The Big Brain at the Heart of the Matter

Why did we evolve brains with the largest prefrontal cortex in the animal kingdom? That old adage that humans use only 10% of their brains seems to come from the fact that much of the prefrontal cortex is barely understood. Indeed, only a few decades ago, prefrontal lobotomies—the surgical severing of the prefrontal cortex from the rest of the brain—were considered viable treatments for mental illness. In other words, "If you don't know what it does, cut it out."

But recent research on executive functions has shown that there is indeed a purpose for the prefrontal cortex. It seems to be the place where complex information is processed—a pooling area where linguistic, emotional, and kinesthetic inputs are processed together to yield the highest-level analysis of which we are capable. The prefrontal cortex, then, is the high-level information-processing organ of the human being.

So what is the nature of the information in which this part of the brain specializes? What is it that makes us truly human and unique?

Certainly it has something to do with language and communication, but chances are it involves other aspects of being human as well. I propose that the true role of the prefrontal cortex is to enable human beings to participate in the fourth kingdom. Each fourth kingdom environment has a set of characteristics that require certain ways of participating. We have referred to these as *roles*, or differentiation and hierarchicalization.

If in the past few thousand years "man the wise" has become "man the communicator," then surely in the last few centuries "man the role-player" (*Homo thespian?*) has become an important participant in society.

The Proliferation of Roles

Roles are the way people differentiate their behavior when interacting with the fourth kingdom.

Each role has a set of rules, expectations, benefits, rewards, sanctions, and constraints. Roles become internalized to some degree with associated sets of behaviors, emotions, fantasies, pleasures, and pains. Roles are multiplying and becoming more complex at a rate that is in step with the coevolution of communication; they are two sides of the same coin, dual manifestations of a single phenomenon.

Information and *communication* are the social glue that holds roles together—the way in which roles become bound to organizations, and individuals to roles.

What are emotions for? They may be the individual manifestation of expressions and feelings that reinforce social roles. Emotions, as much as anything, have a social role that serves to facilitate communication among and reinforce participation in meaning communities.

Figure 13-2 is nothing short of an evolutionary theory of emotions, consistent with biodynamics, that lays the foundation for a human psychology fit for the fourth kingdom. Unfortunately, full development of these ideas must await a more psychologically focused treatment. It would be a distraction at this point from our emphasis on the fourth kingdom.

A Note on Ideotropic Behavior

Being a member of a meaning community is characterized by *ideotropic* behavior. *Ideotropic behavior* refers to behavior enacted around an idea or set of ideas, principles, or values. Religious worship is an example of ideotropic behavior enacted around the idea of the godhead. Nationalism is an example of ideotropic behavior around the concept of nation or state. Warm and fuzzy feelings at the sound of your old alma mater's song or the morning ritual of the company cheer in the film *Startup.com* are likewise examples of ideotropic behavior.

Figure 13-2: Emotions—The Building Blocks of Human Interaction

Emotion (Valence)	Psycholog-ical Onset	Actor (in relation to object)	Social Surroundings (in relation to actor)	Leads to ... (# = emotion)	Action/Result
1. Joy (+)	Slow	→	←	1, 2	Social bonding
2. Interest (+)	Slow	→	●	2, 1	Exploration/ information seeking
3. Surprise (0)	Sudden	●	●	1, 5, 6	Stop/clear
4. Sadness (-)	Slow	●	←	4	Comfort seeking
5. Fear (-)	Sudden	←	→	5, 4, 6	Quick withdrawal
6. Anger (-)	Sudden	→	→	6, 4	Object destruction

7. Disgust (-)	Sudden	⟶	⟵ (social ambivalence)	5, 6, 2	Object avoidance (5, 6) or approach (2, 6)
Complex Emotions	Evolves From				
8. Dominance/ leadership	Anger				
9. Subservience/ followership	Fear				
10. Greed/ acquisitiveness	Interest (+fear)				
11. Passion/ involvement	Joy (+interest)				
12. Intransigence/ stubbornness	Sadness				
13. Social Disgust/ prejudice	Disgust				

⟶ = away from object or emoter

⟷ = ambivalence or indecisiveness

⟵ = toward object or emoter

● = stationary in relation to object or emoter

There are three levels of psychological participation in meaning communities. Level 1 pertains to the most basic, hard-wired motivational programs that we experience as human beings, i.e., emotional participation. Level 2 relates to values, which are associations of emotions with the interpersonal environment, and are somewhat more plastic than the emotions themselves. (The complex emotions in Figure 13-2 fall somewhere between Level 1 and Level 2.)

Level 3 of ideotropic behavior relates to organizational alignment. Organizational alignments are those plastic, nonspecific behaviors that demonstrate oneness of purpose with a fourth kingdom organism. Patriotism, religious devotion, and company loyalty are all examples of organizational alignment.

Homo Neticus—The Face of the Future

It would be difficult to overemphasize the role that information plays in modern society. For this reason, the biodynamic theory of emotions I suggest is, at core, a communication theory of emotions. That is, emotions evolved to communicate information to the social group. Without the proximity of other people, emotions would be unnecessary.

Homo communicans, man the communicator, is giving way to *Homo neticus,* man the networked. As with *Homo neanderthalis* and *Homo sapiens,* they will coexist for a while, but the latter will eventually overtake the former. How and why? *Homo neticus* is plugged in 24/7, often communicating with multiple people simultaneously. Technology has enabled us to become hypercommunicators. The interesting thing about this is that it enables us to juggle many roles at once.

Imagine this scenario: Jane is in a meeting with her coworkers. With her laptop open (she's connected, of course, wirelessly or through one of the ubiquitous ports found in any conference room), she is scrolling through e-mails when an instant message from a friend at another company pops up. While she is engaged in e-mailing and IMing (notice they have both become verbs), her cell phone rings. It is her husband, saying he will be home late. While she is speaking to him, one of her children texts her, requesting that she intervene in a fight with a sibling.

Four or more conversations are occurring simultaneously in this scenario, each as a function of a different role. Colleague, friend, wife, mother—*Homo neticus* increasingly relies on technology to keep her plugged in to the network.

Instant messaging is a particularly interesting phenomenon. I first heard of it several years ago from a friend who was a child therapist. It was a new fad among teens and preteens subscribed to America Online, allowing them to have simultaneous group conversations, sometimes while talking on the telephone to someone else. Then their parents discovered it. While I was preparing the second edition, this chapter seemed both quaint and prescient. With the advent of Facebook, Instagram, texting, and so on, there are now dozens of communication channels, not at all limited to roles.

A November 4, 2002, article in the *Wall Street Journal* stated that even then, about 200 million workers used e-mail, and 75 million computer users took advantage of instant messaging. Although companies tried to stifle the practice for security reasons, *Homo neticus* simply must be on the network communicating, and companies decided to introduce security rather than try to stop the irrepressible urge to IM. Again, add texting, Facebook, Instagram, and so on, not to mention the fact that over a billion devices exist to facilitate all of these communications. Once again, fact is stranger than prediction.

These trends and tendencies are even stronger among younger people. In some Scandinavian countries it is not unusual for 7-year-olds to have cell phones. Go to a restaurant frequented by teens and young adults and notice how many of them think nothing of carrying on a cell phone conversation, texting, and/

or viewing data feeds while dining with friends. Behavior that is considered rude by their parents is perfectly acceptable among peers. And our friend Jane, in the example above, is much more likely to be under 35 than over 45, because the young truly are at home with the newer technologies.

Keep this in mind and recall that when Teilhard de Chardin spoke about the *noosphere*, it was a mystical and somewhat mysterious construct. Yet today we refer to global communications and the global economy as a prosaic fact of everyday life. What happens, however, when everybody is wired to everyone else via the Internet? What will we become when terabytes and more of information are as accessible as a loaf of bread or a cool drink of water? Indeed, while early economies were based on such commodities as water and bread, future economies will likely be based on the creation and sale of information.

Homo neticus is enabled by the information economy and will in turn feed the information economy, which will become even larger and more pervasive. *Homo neticus* will use communication artifacts to participate in the meaning communities that are the essential components of the fourth kingdom. *Homo neticus* is the hard-wired, software-enabled, post-human being who is destined to inherit the planet and indeed the stars.

The question many will have, no doubt, is "What will be left of our humanity?" If this question sounds chilling to some, it need not be.

While there is nothing inherently moral about the fourth kingdom, there is nothing inherently immoral about it either. Nature, in fact, is *metamoral*. Is the lion taking down an antelope in the African savannah evil? Is the mother wasp who lays her eggs in the soft body of a caterpillar, which then gets eaten from the inside out, immoral? Of course not. They are merely enacting their genetic program in order to survive. So it is with life in the fourth kingdom.

Humans, as creators of meaning communities, must establish roles in which there is room for ethical behavior, roles that encourage free will for the purpose of creating a better world. Remember the emotions that make us human—they must be fed and nurtured.

The evolution of law is relevant here. Law has evolved as a set of rules of engagement between individuals and fourth kingdom organisms. It has become an authority to which almost all fourth kingdom organisms are willing to submit. Law may itself evolve into another species of the fourth kingdom, taking its place along with countries, corporations, universities, and religions. Countries and religions may never cede power to a force beyond their control, but history is full of compromise solutions—the UN, for example—that make the possibilities intriguing.

At the heart of it all will be people—behold *Homo neticus*— biologically hard-wired for emotions and culturally programmed for roles, participating in the meaning communities that comprise the fourth kingdom.

Intriguing indeed, and promising of emerging forms and interrelationships that will continue the dance of life evolving.

14

MINDFUL EVOLUTION: THE DAWN OF THE CONSCIOUS CORPORATION

Benefit Corporations and the Evolution of the Enterprise

T he law considers corporations to be equivalent to actual, living, flesh-and-blood persons. Corporations have rights such as free speech, the ability to make and spend their money as they see fit, and tax benefits. Other rights—not quite as applicable to people in the same way but useful for corporations nonetheless—include multinational status, oversight with little accountability or transparency, and little or no restraint in the pursuit of profit. This equivalence of persons and corporations was not an overnight, discontinuous act of judicial overreach. Rather it is the result of centuries of case law leading slowly, inexorably to the current status of corporations as legal persons (Winkler, 2019).

This is the status quo, and its restatement above will cause nary a raised eyebrow in law firms and law schools around the country. In addition, discussions of these and related issues often devolve into political debates and social questions, whether about civil rights, the environment, or cross-border immigration. It would be easy for the casual or uninformed observer to think these questions are mainly about politics. Conservatives and libertarians often believe there should be few, if any, constraints on businesses and corporations. Liberals and social democrats are often more invested in emphasizing dichotomies between people and corporations, with a decided bias toward individuals. The idea of corporate citizens may even be anathema to them.

The underlying thesis of this chapter is that the debate is a red herring and leads nowhere; you have your values and I have mine. Corporations will do what corporations will do, within the confines of a legal system that has become friendlier and friendlier both to their interests and their means. I want to suggest that this is not a political, judicial, or business debate. If corporations are alive, then biological rules apply. Where does this insight lead?

The Biodynamic Worldview

Biodynamics, as stated in earlier chapters, is defined as "a philosophy, perspective, or worldview that includes [previously stated] ... key ideas and entails the belief and commitment that organizations are best understood as living entities" (see "Important Terms" at the end of the first Preface). It is important for our present purposes to understand that this is neither a metaphor nor manner of speaking: it is literally true.

For some, this idea is silly, obscure, or just plain wrong. It may appear naive or, for the more philosophically adept, be seen as a "category error," as Wittgenstein might say. "You can't use the language of biology to discuss the affairs of business," might be the most succinct way to make this objection. Yet at least since the time of social Darwinism, the worlds of business, science, and society have been irreversibly mixed. In fact, the very term "corporation" comes from the Latin word for "body" (*corpus*), perhaps in etymological recognition of the connection between the two concepts. A living body, like a functioning corporation, is literally alive.

To elaborate on the concept of biodynamics (see Table 14-1 for a summary), seven distinct axioms have been suggested to define and further explain its principles. These axioms or principles comprise Dynamic Systems Theory (DST), "a set of theoretical propositions that explains the workings of all complex living systems, from organisms to organizations" (Sirkin, 2004, p. xiii). The axioms that help us describe and work with complex systems deal with the following phenomena associated with all complex systems: multiple levels, boundaries between parts, differentiation of parts, hierarchies of parts and levels, development, growth (internal and external), and change.

To be more specific, *levels*, for example, pertain to the units under consideration as well as the level of discussion. Tissues and organs comprise bodies, and bodies

Axioms of Dynamic Systems Common Characteristics of All Living Systems		
System Component	**Component Description**	**Examples or Elaboration**
1. Levels	Complex systems have multiple levels upon levels	• Cells, tissues, organs • Workers, management, ownership
2. Boundaries	The very identity of a system, its system integrity, depend on them.	• Cell walls • Role definitions—who does what, who is inside
3. Differentiation	Different parts have different functions, a key to adaptation	• Specialization of function or role • Every part can't do every job equally well

4. Hierarchies	Systems often have lead parts to maximize efficiency	• Cell nucleus • Chief executive officer in the context of an organizational chart
5. Development	All systems change over time, often in predictable ways	• Cells grow as part of their natural life • Successful systems tend to grow larger
6. Growth—internal & external	Internal & external resources are metabolized to feed growth and maintain health	• Cells require energy in the form of food • Business organizations require capital to thrive
7. Change	Living systems are essentially unpredictable; due to environmental exigencies, new forms emerge	• From unicellular organisms to multicellular organisms • From for-profit businesses to B-corps
Table 14-1		

comprise a social system or organization. Each level has its own science and language.

Boundaries regulate a system's integrity, determining what is "in" or within the corpus, and what is "without" or external to the entity. What constitutes a system is its parts organized within a boundary of some sort, whether that boundary is a cell membrane or an employment contract.

Differentiation is key to the specialization of parts within a system. In social systems, this usually suggests specified roles for specified functions. *Leadership*, or lead parts, is a ubiquitous aspect of complex systems that increases organization and maximizes efficiency, from a cell nucleus to a CEO. *Development*, as an aspect of complex systems, leads to change over time that is often adaptive in relation to environmental pressures. *Growth* entails the utilization of resources to make an entity or related group of entities, such as a population or an industry, larger.

Finally, *change* in complex systems is often nonlinear. It cannot be predicted as a simple linear function from point A to point B. New forms of organization emerge and often take on lives of their own. One of these nonlinear changes in the ecosystem of corporations and business law—the benefit corporation—is the topic of this chapter.

What's the Problem with Corporations?

The above, somewhat esoteric discussion of corporations as living entities is a prelude that provides both language and concepts to tackle a larger social issue: What is the problem with corporations?

For many in the corporate or business world, the question is a nonstarter. "What problem?" they may ask. A corporation is a social organization, legally recognized as such, with assets it uses to engage in business and to make a profit. If profits flow and the company grows, or at least protects its niche, there is no problem. Slow or anemic growth is a concern for shareholders and management but always within a business context. It's all about profit and loss, and this is essentially a private conversation between management and shareholders; the latter hold the former accountable. However, this accountability is only in terms of the management's fiduciary responsibility to generate profits for shareholders. There are, according to prevailing legal opinion, no other accountabilities for corporate managers (cf. Strine, 2014).

It should be noted that there is some disagreement among legal scholars whether or not corporations are so constrained. They can in fact, according to these scholars, act in alignment with their fiduciary responsibilities while keeping other considerations beside profit foremost in their decision making (cf. Stout, 2012; Blair & Stout, 1999; Elhauge, 2005). As Strine (2014), who is the chief justice of the Delaware Chancery Court, the court in the US that often sets precedents for corporate law in other states, has written:

> In other words, they argue that managers should "do the right thing," while ignoring that in the current corporate accountability structure, stockholders are the only constituency given any enforceable rights, and thus are the only one with substantial influence over managers. Few commentators have proposed real solutions that would give corporate managers more ability and greater incentives to consider the interests of other constituencies. (p. 235)

Corporations and their managers are duty-bound to maximize profit—period.

A corporation is a legal entity governed by a board of directors (its "leading parts" as referenced above in Axiom 4 of Dynamic Systems Theory, with the chairman of the board as the leading part of the leading part—see Chapter Two). But boards are fiduciaries, who are required to act in the best interests of shareholders, over and above all other interests (Strine, 2014). What are the ramifications of this? If a corporation must decide, for example, whether to legally pollute a river or sacrifice profits, it must—within legal constraints—choose to maximize profits. Substitute any other activity in place of "pollute": dismiss from employment, clear-cut a mountain top, outsource jobs to another city or country, raise the price of a drug by hundreds of percent—the yardstick of shareholder interest, especially short-term interest, is financial. The directors as a group are legally obligated to make decisions that increase shareholder value.

A cautionary note or two: first, corporations are incorporated under state law and are often obligated by that law, which is to say they cannot do whatever they want, whenever they want. Even corporations are constrained by laws. However, there are ways around these minimal constraints. If corporations are multinational, they can sometimes pick and choose the laws they want to obey by redomiciling to a friendlier country or creating legal subsidiaries governed by other laws. An American company with foreign subsidiaries doing business in countries with lax environmental laws, for example, may legally choose to do something in one place that would be illegal someplace else.

A second caveat is that the deep pockets that many corporations bring to bear to protect their self-interest often lead to unfair results, regardless of concerns about social or environmental justice. For example, the dramatic but legal rise of some drug prices recently demonstrates that the "right thing" for investors may not be the "right thing" for a patient who can no longer afford the drugs they need (Smith, 2016).

Imagine that you are a corporation that wants to move. You have been the lifeblood of a town for as long as anyone can remember. Moving will cause significant disruption to this town, its citizens, and your employees, who have been loyal to your company for generations, offering tax breaks and other benefits to you since your earliest days. Management and the board of directors (BOD), if executing their fiduciary responsibility properly, need not, and perhaps should not, consider any factor other than the profitability of the move.

As anyone who reads the newspapers knows, this is not simply a theoretical discussion; rather it is part of the regular conversation among BODs throughout the world. The reasons may vary, but the underlying considerations are usually similar, with consequences beyond the bottom line rarely mentioned, let alone seriously considered. So why is this a problem? It is simply business as usual.

What Kind of Person Is a Corporation?

Imagine for a moment a society in which individual people are motivated by a single concern only: the concern to maximize wealth as they define it. Every decision is made based on the single question, *Does this make me richer?* Friendship, loyalty, social benefit, and harm to others (that does not entail the violation of existing laws) are all secondary to making a profit.

No doubt such people exist. In fact, there is a term for them—we call them "antisocial" (or "psychopathic" or even "sociopathic") personalities (depending on which diagnostic manual we use, and the year it was published, cf. American Psychiatric Association, 2013). These are not necessarily criminals, per se. They are simply individuals concerned with their own needs and desires and with no concern for the needs or feelings of others. It is significant that the ultimate arbiter of mental illness, the DSM-5, chooses to categorize this type of behavior as psychopathology, specifically, a personality disorder which is a type of mental disorder characterized by disordered social relations (American Psychiatric Association, 2013). This is the authoritative guide used by all mental health professionals—psychiatrists, psychologists, social workers, mental health counselors, and psychotherapists of every stripe—to diagnose mental disorders. If corporations are people, there is strong evidence to suggest that they are mentally disordered people.

It is important to realize that one can be psychopathic without being a criminal; not everything immoral is illegal. However, this is precisely the problem, since many or most of the activities of a corporation may not be subject to legal consequences or oversight in exactly the same way that not every action by a person is subject to legal scrutiny. But are we guilty of Wittgenstein's category error again by conflating psychopathological personalities with companies that are bad corporate actors? I think not.

One may wonder if corporations are trying to have their cake and eat it too. They want the benefits of citizenship without any of the responsibilities that come with citizenship. We may be crossing over into moral territory here, perhaps even touching on religion, another type of social organization (Sirkin, 2004). But religions directly address morality and typically hold people to higher standards than "not breaking any laws." In other words, that is the lowest possible bar. While it may be tolerable to have a neighbor who doesn't break any laws, if that were one's only criterion, that neighbor would certainly leave something to be desired. In my town, that neighbor could play loud music or run noisy equipment from 8 a.m. to 11 p.m., burn foul-smelling materials at all hours, and spank—but not technically abuse—his children and pets, and many other activities besides, without any legal recourse on my part. We are discussing "doing the right things" as different from "not breaking any laws."

What Makes a Corporation Happy?

To be sure, some people believe such a world is not just the norm, it is a laudable achievement. A philosophy that reflects the values of Nietzsche (power) and Rand (unfettered capitalism); that lionizes power and money respectively; that demonstrates an open disdain for the weak, powerless, and poor is a philosophy that gives succor to its most egregious corporate citizens.

Yet we live in a society that was founded on the inalienable rights of people to "life, liberty, and the pursuit of happiness." The founders may have perhaps—though probably not—meant to include corporate citizens here. Problematically, American case law has evolved, with the help of the best corporate lawyers money could buy over the last 100-plus years, to allow corporate "people" to do things that harm others (Winkler, 2019). Corporations, according to Delaware and US law, seem to have been granted life and liberty. Does it make sense to talk about a corporation's "pursuit of happiness"?

We are approaching the crux of the problem. On some level, it makes no sense at all to talk about a corporation's happiness. We know intuitively, if no other way, that happiness applies to flesh-and-blood people, not corporations, and probably entails the triggering of emotions (cf. Harari, 2017, for an in-depth discussion of the role of emotions, not just cognition, in making us uniquely human). No one, to my knowledge, has yet held that corporations have emotions. Yet many if not most corporations do have vision and mission statements. Could these suffice as operational definitions of the pursuit of happiness for a corporation? Certainly they represent corporate values. Let us allow that even if corporations can't feel, they can still want or desire certain outcomes in line with their values.

Perhaps "happiness" is too high a bar. After all, if we are serious about our biological or biodynamic approach, we will have difficulty answering what makes an animal or plant happy. We typically use language such as "health" or "illness" to describe thriving creatures or sick ones. Nature has few rules, and the ones we typically use are short and brutal: "eat or be eaten," Tennyson's "red in tooth and claw," and of course the shibboleth of Darwinian evolution, "survival of the fittest."

Herein lies the crux of our problem. Dumb creatures—all animate life forms, actually—need to survive both as individuals and species. If there is an obvious meaning or purpose to life, this must be it to some degree or other. As a scientist, I find this easy to believe because I see the proof of it every day in the natural world. As a sentient being, however—as a person—I see there is more to life than survival and procreation.

Growth, unchecked, is problematic. Populations in nature achieve dynamic equilibrium; that is, they grow until outside constraints, typically a lack of resources such as space or food, prevent further growth, or even lead to shrinkage. Growth resumes once external conditions have improved (Axiom 6, see Table 14-1). This is how we have come to understand how ecosystems grow and change, yet remain the same within the parameters of change. That is what dynamic equilibrium achieves.

The classic example is the wolf and hare populations in a grassland ecosystem. One goes up and the other goes down, yet they are correlated in dynamic equilibrium, achieving a long-term balance. Too many hares and the wolves increase and eat them, leading to more wolves and fewer hares. Too many wolves leads to not enough hares. The wolves must then migrate or starve, either way reducing the population of wolves. This makes it safer for hares to procreate, and so they do. Every dynamic ecosystem works in the same way to achieve balance or stasis.

Corporations too survive in economic ecosystems we call industries; and the sum total of all economic activity gives us local and world economies (Sirkin, 2004). Survival in the corporate world is competitive. Darwin's survival of the fittest seems to be the law of all biological organisms, whether they be cellular, multicellular, personal, or multipersonal.

Corporations are multipersonal organisms. They are made up of constituent parts, some more or less essential than others, but all together are the organism. This organism vies with other organisms in its ecosystem to survive, grow, and thrive. Perhaps this is as good as it gets, and corporations, like wolf populations or algal blooms, cannot hope for more and should not expect more. Yet people do expect more, want more, need more in order to have a fulfilling life. Perhaps it is this notion of "fulfilling," with the implication of values, higher truths, beauty, and service for the greater good, that creates a dilemma. Perhaps "happiness" is fulfillment, and we just don't know what that means in a corporate context. One can almost hear the corporations on the couch, sighing with existential angst. "Doc, there must be more to life than profits, profits, profits." Or perhaps we will find this corporation in the confessional, asking or praying, "Forgive me, Father, for I have sinned."

I don't know what makes a corporation happy. Not many people have asked. Most, I fear, would find the question nonsensical, a nonstarter, a basic category error, imputing feelings and aspirations to a conglomeration of bricks-and-mortar and people and processes that constitute the modern corporation. Yet what then can it mean to call a corporation a person, with the rights our legal system grants to all persons? If corporations are people— and the reader should remember this is not really open to debate; from the legal standpoint, this is settled case law—we as a society grant them rights. But, as for all citizens, with those rights come responsibilities.

And the law recognizes this too. There are many laws that constrain corporations: laws against monopolies and other unfair trade practices, laws about how to treat workers, laws about taxes, and so on. Laws are one aspect of external constraint. Competition is another. Being a corporation is a tough life, it would seem, one in which the price of a misstep can be reductions in share price, takeovers, or bankruptcy. Perhaps life is war, and it really is "nasty, brutish, and short" (Hobbes, 1651/2018).

On Being a Better Corporation

Beyond existence and survival, as people we aspire for more. We want to be happy or fulfilled, to live our lives for something, to be for something. This is where values, whether they be religious, existential, or simply humanitarian, come into play. As humans, we seem to want and need more than a nasty, brutish existence. Education, government, and religion are three social institutions that enable people to come together to accomplish these goals or at least strive toward them.

Earlier in this book, I have suggested that the planet has given rise, over the past dozen millennia, to four types of multipersonal, self-organizing classes of dynamic systems: religions, governments, colleges, and corporations (see "Important Terms" at the end of the first Preface). Think of each as a species of multipersonal organism. Without going into the nature, similarities, and differences of each, for our purposes we may view them all as living systems. Through their interactions, they form multipersonal ecosystems, or society. Among the goals of these institutions, the "betterment" or improvement of individuals is among the most salient. Whether through education or religious devotion, a general goal of our social institutions is to improve society by setting higher standards for people and enabling them to live up to those standards, whether materially or mentally or both.

Government contributes to this goal, in one sense, by reducing the ability of people to interfere with or impinge on others. Government has also taken to offering rewards, in the form of cash and benefits, to encourage positive behavior that translates into greater good for greater numbers (a utilitarian approach as, suggested by Bentham, 1781/1988). These benefits may include tax breaks, government contracts, and other emoluments that encourage or reward companies for pro-social behavior.

In this vein, the saying "Man does not live by bread alone" suggests a corporate corollary: "Businesses do not live by profit alone." There is no imperative here. This is not what *must* be, only what we choose. Although morality is an aesthetic choice or, as Kant suggests, a moral imperative, the fact that we know the difference and believe we are capable of choice places us in a moral dilemma. The wolf doesn't exactly choose to eat the hare but does so as a function of its biological imperatives. A person who kills another person, however, absent good reason such as self-defense or survival, has a choice. And society holds them responsible for that choice. This is what we mean when we call a person a moral agent.

Corporations, I suggest, can also be moral agents, because they can act with self-awareness and intent. However, for a variety of reasons, our society has relatively low standards for morality when it comes to corporate behavior. Corporations, rather than being aspirational, are minimalist—they are expected to do the minimum, or less, to be "good enough" corporate citizens.

Some may argue with this assumption, citing circumstances in which reputation or good citizenship rewards a corporation with more business success and higher profits. Also, companies that flagrantly flaunt or actively work against the social good may find themselves in a public relations nightmare. This could negatively impact profits, which may indirectly cause a change in behavior. But short of the negative impact on profits, few public companies would seriously consider, let alone feel forced to change from barely meeting standards to exceeding them.

Profits Über Alles

As discussed above, a typical corporation with shareholders must, by law, maximize profits for the benefit of its shareholders. Profit can, and usually does, trump every other consideration. It is the ultimate justification for any action, however repugnant such action may be. One egregious example should suffice:

> In 2015 Valeant acquired the heart drug Isuprel and promptly raised the price for a single vial from $440 to $2,700, citing a responsibility to shareholders to maximize profit. This 600% increase would have cost our hospital $1.6 million each year and forced us to remove it from emergency crash carts. (Smith, 2016)

The brouhaha over this corporate behavior was instructive: the business press rationalized the company's "profits first" behavior, while physicians' groups, hospitals, and the general public painted a more diabolical picture (Smith, 2016; Davis, 2016). Interestingly, Davis appealed not to ethics or laws, but to the "magic" of market forces to make these companies do the right thing:

> Companies that seek to exploit the pharmaceutical business solely to maximize their own profit without regard to patient needs must be humbled by the very force they have sought to avoid—the market-correcting power of supply and demand. (Davis, 2016)

However, like the good capital machines they were designed to be, the pharma companies guilty of these practices richly rewarded their shareholders, who seemed to have few objections to these practices which made them lots of money. One such company, Turing, as a private entity, was not even subject to shareholder opprobrium. At the opposite extreme, the CEO of Valeant was forced to resign. Regardless, the business model is profitable. These companies, while seeking to manage whatever PR problems their actions cause, seem to have no good reason, using the shareholder value standard, to change their behavior in any substantial way.

Further, I would suggest this is not an isolated instance. Whether the bad behavior is about worker safety (the mining industry), environmental pollution (the petroleum industry), or consumer safety (the tobacco industry), companies regularly and systematically do what they can get away with to maximize profit. Corporations, and the people who work in them, are socialized from earliest times that companies exist to make money for their owners, the more the better. Any other considerations that affect that prime directive are naive, unrealistic, or in some cases actually illegal.

Recently, a former corporate lawyer has taken this case one step further. James Gamble (2016) has gone so far as to call profit maximization the most important problem in the world today. Beginning with the recognition of the unparalleled power of corporations, he goes on to reason that an entity with this much power can and does wreak havoc in the world. He suggests, somewhat less convincingly, that the solution is for companies to adopt binding codes of conduct. Let us leave that potential solution for another discussion, while accepting the dire problems created by profit maximization at any cost.

A New Type of Company

By now, the reader should realize that profits are not just a pleasant byproduct of a company or business; they are its raison d'être. Financial profitability is part of the DNA of the modern company. It is why they exist, why people invest in them, and what they are for. If the goal is to have a company that can at least aspire to some sort of moral behavior (or morally aware behavior), we must consider changing the very DNA that makes a company what it is.

Profit and the pursuit of it are no small things. It may reasonably be argued that corporations, in one form or another, make the modern world possible. In truth, it is corporations in conjunction with educational, governmental, and religious institutions that have made the modern world possible. Our current world is healthier, smarter, richer, and probably more moral than at any previous point in history (Pinker, 2011). Every modern convenience, from mobile phones and computers to airplanes and cars, has been developed and is manufactured and sold by corporations. It is simply a fact that the economic system that undergirds our modern world is only possible because of corporations, and corporations only exist, except in rare instances, to make a profit.

It is not the profit motive itself that is problematic. It is the profit motive as prime—in most cases sole—directive that creates the problems. Indeed, there are laws that make hybrid entities possible, such as the not-for-profit corporation or its close cousin, the NGO (non-governmental agency). Not-for-profits do great good in the world, but they are essentially charities, with no intention of making a profit and in most cases not legally entitled to hold on to profits when they do. Profit and charity, in the world of corporate law, seem to be opposed.

Multiple Bottom Lines

It is often said, "One can only manage what one can measure. Corporate managers, in their quest to perfect processes that ensure profits, have sought to measure things in addition to profitability. That is, if profitability is the desired output, what are the relevant inputs? It is only through measurement and documentation, over time, that we can really understand what contributes to the bottom line of profitability.

The idea of the balanced scorecard introduced or built upon the idea of multiple bottom lines (Kaplan & Norton, 1992, 1996). Managers may choose to measure many things for many reasons, and the idea of keeping score was an innovative and exciting development for managers. While the balanced scorecard provided a means, it did not provide the why. Kaplan and Norton (1992) were accountants seeking new ways to measure and improve business processes. Around the same time, Elkington introduced the idea of sustainability for corporations (Elkington, 1997), which he captured in the notion of the triple bottom line (TBL): profits, people, and planet (the three Ps). The traditional bottom line of profit now must share the stage with other (equally?) important business outcomes. These include the effect the company has on people—typically its employees, but also workers in the supply chain and consumers—and the effect the company has on the environment, in all its relevant manifestations (see Figure 14-1).

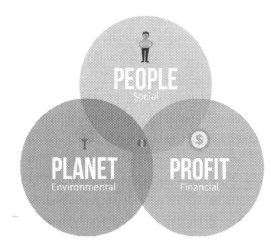

Source: https://cdn-images-1.medium.com/
max/1600/0*MlgHOkWU23krNzvg
Figure 14-1
Triple Bottom Line:
People, Planet, Profit

TBL is more than just an accounting practice. It offers a business philosophy and a way to measure it. It says, in effect, that in every company there are at least three bottom lines, and enlightened management needs to measure and be accountable for all three. These bottom lines, in turn, are composite and have many components that also need to be measured. The emphasis is on sustainability, which requires attention to all three bottom lines.

Recently, Elkington (2018) has critiqued the movement because it has become a mere accounting tool rather than the vanguard of a movement to change corporate values.

Industry Standard – Concept of *Triple Bottom-line*

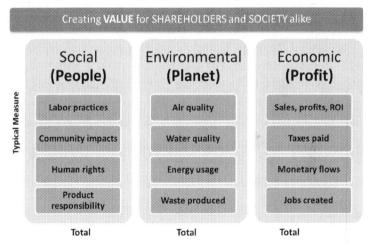

Source: http://csr-csss.blogspot.com/
Figure 14-2
Details of the Triple Bottom Line

The Advent of the Benefit Corporation

The importance of creating sustainable, triple-P companies has become increasingly urgent. The modern corporation needs to be not only profitable for shareholders and therefore able to attract investors, but also people-friendly to attract motivated and skilled workers without harming its customers and planet-friendly to sustain the environment and husband natural resources. Indeed, while I was writing this chapter, 180 CEOs from the American Business Roundtable called on their members to be more purpose driven, and less profit driven (*The Economist*, 2019). *The Economist*, a conservative, pro-business, pro-profit magazine, took a dim view of the CEOs' initiative. They preferred to trust the economics of competition over the well-meaning plans of some do-gooder CEO. The editors announced the plan DOA, choosing blind faith in Smith's invisible hand to lead corporations to do good, despite all evidence to the contrary.

The Inherent Conundrum of Profit

Traditional corporations, by putting financial profit first, put other important factors second or third or fourth. Factors such as good citizenship in the community, wise husbandry of natural resources, and worker well-being all come after considerations of profit. Hard-core capitalists believe there is nothing wrong with this. They believe that a company is like a self-correcting machine and the complex economics of corporations and industries will, in the long run, punish bad behavior (Smith, 1776/2016).

Although this may be true sometimes, even often, there are many instances when it is not. Philip Morris and other tobacco companies paid a high price for killing their consumers. However, after paying, they went back to being profitable with an added push into international markets that didn't have such pesky rules about products that kill people. Adam Smith's invisible hand did not save the tens of millions of people who died and who continue to be sickened by tobacco products. And so it goes, whether we are talking about oil and coal polluters, minimum-wage employees who can't support themselves with full-time work, and so on. These unfortunate events occur because these companies are not designed to make consumers or environments healthy. They exist to make a profit for shareholders.

Although the topic is not fashionable to discuss in some circles, many feel the government is the lynchpin in a system of checks and balances that keeps corporate "bad behavior" under control. But these systems are imperfect for several reasons. First, they can usually only act after some malfeasance is committed; rarely can they be proactive. Second, the deep pockets of companies often allow them to drag out court cases for decades and/or get fines reduced so that the penalties are diluted to the point of ineffectiveness. Finally, prosecution as well as malfeasance are often subject to which way the political winds are blowing. A conservative, pro-corporate administration may be reluctant to enforce rules or exact meaningful penalties from corporate criminals.

The attitude of many companies is that it's not a crime unless they're caught—and even then there are ways to wriggle out of the legal consequences. Beside that, one cannot put a corporation in jail. And just to add insult to injury, any legal penalties are tax deductible—simply the cost of doing business and breaking laws in a complex world. The government and the political class seem unequal to the task of policing the world's corporations.

So governments can't stop corporations, and they can't seem to stop themselves. Market forces, while powerful, also seem inadequate when it comes to companies behaving badly. As we have seen above, it would not be incorrect to think of corporations as psychopathic in the sense they do not consider the best interests of others, only themselves. Corporations may express some contrition, perhaps, if caught, but no they demonstrate no true moral compass allowing them to evaluate right from wrong. After all, "right" is when you make a profit—and you know you are right because Wall Street rewards you with high valuations and big bonuses for management.

The stage is set for the benefit corporation, or B corp, to make its entrance stage left.

What Is a Benefit Corporation (B Corp)?

Traditional corporations are expected to use profit maximization as the primary lens through which to view corporate decision-making (Strine, 2014). However, some now see this as a hurdle in creating long-term value for all stakeholders, including the shareholders themselves. Quarterly profitability goals, beloved by Wall Street, may in fact be detrimental to long-term viability or success.

Benefit corporations reject a profit-centric model of corporate governance. Rather, they are required to consider all stakeholders in their decisions. This gives them the flexibility to create long-term value for all stakeholders.

According to corporate law in the United States, as upheld by the Delaware Chancery Court, corporations are required to maximize profit for their shareholders (Strine, 2014). Changing this mandate requires changing the laws under which corporations are created. Traditional corporations are called "C corporations," and they must, by law, maximize profit. The ideas behind benefit corporation, or B corps, are to create legal corporations that benefit the public in some specified way and are also entitled to make a profit. However, and explicitly, making a profit is not the ultimate and certainly not the only way for a B corp to be successful. Each state must adopt laws making B corps legal. To date, approximately 34 states have laws allowing B corps, and another six are in process of legalization.

In addition, to be part of this movement, it is not enough to incorporate as a B corp. These companies are held to a higher standard and must submit to regular B corp assessments, which result in the company's official certification as a B corp. A B corp assessment looks at several discrete areas and a number of categories within each area—for example, government, workers, community, and environment. Each category and subcategory must be reported and scored, and the company must achieve a minimal score to be certified as a B corp. Further, the report must be made public, thereby reinforcing a core value of these companies: transparency.

While B corps may be a blueprint for a new type of company, the blueprint itself is grounded in a philosophy of interdependence that is not incompatible with Dynamic Systems Theory. In this view, corporations are part of a larger, natural world characterized by the interconnectedness of all social systems. The movement's declaration of interdependence is quite explicit in envisioning a world in which business is a force for good. Companies are purpose driven and create "benefit for all stakeholders, not just shareholders" (see Figure 14-3). The keystone "species" of business organization they envision in this new world is the B corp. The B corp movement introduces an explicit moral dimension in the conduct of its business, such that:

- All business ought to be conducted as if people and place matter.
- Through their products, practices, and profits, businesses should aspire to do no harm and to benefit all.
- A sense of mutual responsibility should guide corporate thinking with respect to current and future generations.

Put simply, a benefit corporation is a new legal entity that creates a solid foundation for long-term mission alignment and value creation.

It protects the mission through (or despite) multiple capital raises and leadership changes, creates more flexibility when evaluating potential sale and liquidity options, and prepares businesses to lead a mission-driven life post-IPO. A benefit corporation is a traditional corporation with modified obligations committing it to higher standards of purpose, accountability, and transparency.

In terms of purpose, benefit corporations commit to creating public benefit and sustainable value in addition to generating profit. This sustainability is an integral part of their value proposition. In terms of accountability, benefit corporations are committed to considering the company's impact on society and the environment in order to create long-term sustainable value for all stakeholders. Finally, in terms of transparency, benefit corporations are required to report, in most states annually and using a third party standard, showing their progress towards achieving beneficial social and environmental impact.

Figure 14-3

The B Corp Declaration of Interdependence

We envision a global economy that uses business as a force for good.

This economy is comprised of a new type of corporation—the B Corporation—Which is purpose-driven and creates benefit for all stakeholders, not just shareholders.

As B Corporations and leaders of this emerging economy, we believe:

- That we must be the change we seek in the world.
- That all business ought to be conducted as if people and place mattered.
- That, through their products, practices, and profits, businesses should aspire to do no harm and benefit all.
- To do so requires that we act with the understanding that we are each dependent upon another and thus responsible for each other and future generations.

(Retrieved 09/03/2019 from About B Corps. from https://bcorporation.net/about-b-corps

Currently, according to the website www.bcorporation.net, there are almost 3,000 B corps in 64 countries, spanning 150 industries. As of September 2019, B corps may be the brightest hope on the corporate horizon. The movement has been working hard to build members, credibility, and processes. Recent developments such as articles by Gamble (2019), front-page stories in *The Economist* (Editor, 2019), and the CEO announcement generated by the American Business Roundtable all point to a realization that something needs changing. Add to this presidential candidate Elizabeth Warren's recent call to create federal charters for corporations in order to hold them to higher (purpose-driven) standards, and we see a movement gathering a head of steam. But we have a long way to go before B corps become the norm or any of these other suggestions are adopted wholesale.

Conclusions

In the last months of 2019, the world is more aware than ever that corporations are big, powerful, and may represent multiple levels of threat to our way of life. A prominent attorney calls them, or at least their unethical behavior, "the biggest problem in the world" (Gamble, 2019). As with other complex, living systems, companies have evolved from simple businesses to multinational conglomerates. With that evolution comes money, power, mass destruction of resources, and the ability to dictate terms to millions of customers and workers.

From the unique biological vantage point of DST, we understand this evolution as natural and to some extent predictable. Large complex systems become larger and more complex in order to command and control resources. Their subsequent success encourages greater growth and additional complexity. Life on earth has been a slow-motion arms race for 2.5 billion years, and it shows no signs of letting up anytime soon. In fact, with the advent of big data, smart cities, artificial intelligence, and the internet of things, companies are using technology to coevolve with and, in some cases, surpass human functioning. Harari (2019) predicts that within 100 years, AI algorithms will literally run the world. If companies can function better without humans, there is no reason to think they won't someday. Taking a page from evolutionary biology, if those companies are more "fit," i.e., more efficient, more profitable, and more successful, then why wouldn't they surpass their competitors in every way?

So it is possible that we humans will become relegated to an impotent or unimportant status, like dung beetles on the African savannah. Yes, they do stuff, but no one considers them a keystone species there. That is one potential outcome: as a species, we become less and less relevant as our bigger and more complex "children" take over the world. Our place may be to function as an integral part of their function, as cells within larger bodies do.

No one knows what this will look like, and the outcomes lie hundreds, if not thousands, of years in the future. I do not see this as a nightmare scenario, where we become cogs in an unthinking and unaware machine à la the Matrix. Rather these will be relationships similar to others in the animal and plant world as we explore variations of mutualism, commensalism, parasitism, and other ways of coexisting.

Today, in this volume, we have identified four potential types or species of complex living systems: corporations, governments, religions, and universities. More species of the fourth kingdom will no doubt evolve. Even if this evolution happens relatively quickly in planetary time, it will take many human lifetimes to unfold. This, in some sense, was my original thinking in the first edition in 2004. Yet there is an alternative on the horizon, and it is worth serious exploration.

The idea of large, self-sufficient corporate organisms is frightening primarily because our models of living systems in relationship are limited: eat-or-be-eaten (e.g., predation or cannibalism), mutual benefit (e.g., mutualism or commensalism), or some variations on these themes. Another alternative is some sort of incorporation, in which the parts come together to form an entity greater than any part. As discussed elsewhere, the evolutionary biologist Lynn Margulis (2002) has speculated that multicellular organisms evolved in just this way, as a "joint venture" among several simpler, single-celled organisms. A long whiplike creature becomes the flagellum of a larger single-celled organism. The ability to metabolize organic chemicals become the cell's mitochondria. Such mutually beneficial specializations continued to evolve until, like Frankenstein's monster, a creature emerged from the parts.

In his first book, *Sapiens*, Yuval Noah Harari (2015) tells us that the key to human evolution and worldwide dominance is our ability to tell stories. I do not disagree. From this one ability (a genetic mutation near Broca's area in the human brain, perhaps?), everything uniquely human stems: values, philosophy, religion, education, commerce, nationalism, and so on. Culture is a story, nationalism is a story, religion is a story, education is a story, and commerce is a story.

Further, the ability to tell moral stories—stories in which fairness and equity play an important role—has enabled us to work together to create joint projects and endeavors. Our stories about moral agents, whether they be in the Bible or the laws of incorporation, describe characters that have moral agency. These agents make decisions that impact the world. It may well be humanity's role is to make corporations moral agents. This is an alternative future to mindless evolution. Call it "mindful evolution," and humanity can influence corporations to adopt it, use it, and have it become an essential ingredient of a new corporate form.

We've seen the beginnings of this in the B corp movement, in which society, corporate members, and other companies have begun to think about a world and the companies who inhabit it as moral agents. We are at the early stages, but this approach holds promise. We have a responsibility to socialize corporations in the same sense that a culture has a responsibility to socialize its children—whether this is done through the language of incorporation (special B corps), corporate bylaws, or other methods.

The world is painfully aware that corporations, in their current C form, are not ethical players at best, and are psychopaths (or antisocial personalities) at worst. Most of us would not choose to live with a psychopath, and only a fool would give an amoral agent power over him or her. We have been fools, but at least we are waking up to the fact. Once awake, perhaps we can even fix it.

Corporations are complex creatures trying to survive and thrive; they're just trying to make a living. But respecting the rights and freedoms of others is paramount to the good life in a functional society. This means treating others fairly, not taking things without paying for them, and not taking advantage of the commons we all share. It will take all the other fourth kingdom denizens to accomplish the great task of socializing corporations so, rather than simply maximize profit, they maximize the good on multiple levels (as with the multiple bottom line approaches). States must pass and enforce laws that hold companies accountable; religions must look beyond the individual or coreligionists to other life forms that should be treated fairly; and education must take a lead in teaching future business leaders that companies cannot and should not function without ethical guidance and moral responsibilities.

How this all evolves will take many years and is beyond anyone's guess at the present. But evolve it must, since this is the only story humanity has left.

REFERENCES

About B Corps. (2019, September 12). Retrieved from https://bcorporation.net/about-b-corps

Agazarian, Y. M. (1982). Role as a bridge construct in understanding the relationship between the individual and the group. In M. Pines & M. Rafelson (Eds.), *The individual and the group: Boundaries and interrelations* (pp. 68–79). New York, NY: Plenum.

Agazarian, Y. M. (1992). A systems approach to the group-as-a-whole. *International Journal of Group Psychotherapy, 42*, 3–12.

Alderfer, C. P. (1977). Group and intergroup relations. In H. Hackman, J. Richard, & J. Suttle (Eds.), *Improving life at work* (pp. 227–296). Santa Monica, CA: Goodyear.

Alderfer, C. P. (1986). An intergroup perspective on group dynamics. In J. Lorsch (Ed.), *Handbook of organizational behavior* (pp. 190–222). Englewood Cliffs, NJ: Prentice-Hall.

Allport, G. W. (1955). *Becoming: Basic considerations for a psychology of personality.* New Haven, CT: Yale University Press.

Allport, G. W. (1961). *Pattern and growth in personality.* New York, NY: Holt, Rinehart and Winston.

American Psychiatric Association. (2017). *Diagnostic and statistical manual of mental disorders: DSM-5*. Arlington, VA: Author.

Argyris, C., & Schon, D. A. (1978). *Organizational learning: A theory of action perspective*. Reading, MA: Addison-Wesley.

Bandler, R., & Grinder, J. (1975). *The structure of magic: A book about language and therapy*. Palo Alto, CA: Science and Behavior Books.

Bateson, G. (1972). *Steps to an ecology of mind*. New York, NY: Ballantine Books.

Bateson, G. (1979). *Mind and nature: A necessary unity*. New York, NY: E. P. Dutton.

Bateson, G., & Ruesch, J. (1951). *Communication: The social matrix of psychiatry*. New York, NY: W. W. Norton.

Becker, B., Huselid, M., & Ulrich, D. (1999). *The HR scorecard: Linking people, strategy, and performance*. Cambridge, MA: Harvard Business Press.

Bentham, J. (1988). *Introduction to the principles of morals and legislation*. Amherst, NY: Prometheus Books. (Originally published in 1781).

Berlinski, D. (1976). *On systems analysis: An essay concerning the limitations of some mathematical methods in the social, political, and biological sciences*. Cambridge, MA: The MIT Press.

Bion, W. R. (1959). *Experiences in groups, and other papers*. *London, United Kingdom*: Tavistock.

Bion, W. R. (1961). *Experiences in groups*. London, United Kingdom: Tavistock.

Blair, M. M. & Lynn A. Stout, L. A. (1999). A team production theory of corporate law, 85 *Virginia Law Review*, 247, 253.

Borwick, I. (1986). The family therapist as business consultant. In L. C. Wynne, S. H. McDaniel, & T. T. Weber (Eds.), *Systems consultation: A new perspective for family therapy* (pp. 423–440). New York, NY: The Guilford Press.

Boulding, K.E. (1966). *Economic analysis* (4th ed.). New York, NY: Harper & Row.

Carter, B., & McGoldrick, M. (Eds.). (1989). *The changing family life cycle: A framework for family therapy* (2nd ed.). New York, NY: W. W. Norton.

Christiansen, C. (1997). *The innovator's dilemma: When new technologies cause great firms to fail*. Cambridge, MA: Harvard University Press.

Clippinger, J. H., III (Ed.). (1999). *The biology of business: Decoding the natural laws of enterprise*. San Francisco, CA: Jossey-Bass.

Collins, J. (2001). *Good to great: Why some companies make the leap … and others don't*. New York, NY: Harper Collins.

Davis, K. L. (2016, June 3). Price gougers like Valeant Pharmaceuticals must be tamed. Forbes. Retrieved from https://www.forbes.com/sites/kennethdavis/2016/06/03/a-market-fix-for-generic-drug-price-gouging/#650d0e6d6f21

De Geus, A. P. (1997). *The living company.* Cambridge, MA: Harvard University Press.

Denning, S. (2001). *The springboard: How storytelling ignites action in knowledge-era organizations.* Boston, MA: Butterworth, Heinemann.

Diamond, J. (1997). *Guns, germs, and steel: The fates of human societies.* New York, NY: W. W. Norton.

Editor. (2019, August 22). What companies are for. *The Economist.* Retrieved from https://www.economist.com/leaders/2019/08/22/what-companies-are-for

Elhauge, E. (2005). Corporate managers' operational discretion to sacrifice corporate profits in the public interest. In H. Bruce, R. Stavins, & R. Vietor (Eds.), *Environmental protection and the social responsibility of firms.* Washington, DC: Resources for the Future.

Elkington, J. (1997). Cannibals with forks: The triple bottom line of 21st century business. *Capstone.*

Elkington, J. (2018, June 25). 25 years ago I coined the phrase "Triple Bottom Line." Here's why it's time to rethink it. *Harvard Business Review.*

Ekman, P. (2003). *Emotions revealed: Recognizing faces and feelings to improve communication and emotional life.* New York, NY: Times Books.

Eldredge, N. (1985). *Time frames: The rethinking of Darwinian evolution and the theory of punctuated equilibria.* New York, NY: Simon and Schuster.

Eldredge, N., & Gould, S. J. (1972). Punctuated equilibria: An alternative to phyletic gradualism. In T. J. Schopf (Ed.), *Models in paleobiology* (pp. 82–115). San Francisco, CA: Freeman, Cooper.

Ellenberger, H. F. (1970). *The discovery of the unconscious: The history and evolution of dynamic psychiatry.* New York, NY: Basic Books.

Engel, G. (1980). The clinical application of the biopsychosocial model. *American Journal of Psychiatry, 137,* 535–544.

Fitz-enz, J. (2000). *The ROI of human capital: Measuring the economic value of employee performance.* New York, NY: AMACOM.

Forrester, J. W. (1968). *Principles of systems.* Cambridge, MA: Pegasus Communications.

Freud, S. (1950). *Totem and taboo: Some points of agreement between the mental lives of savages and neurotics* (J. Strachey, Ed. and Trans.). New York, NY: W. W. Norton. (Original work published 1913)

Freud, S. (1959). *Group psychology and the analysis of the ego* (J. Strachey, Ed. and Trans.). New York, NY: W. W. Norton. (Original work published 1921)

Gamble, J. (2019, March 13). The most important problem in the world - James Gamble ... Retrieved from https://medium.com/@jgg4553542/the-most-important-problem-in-the-world-ad22ade0ccfe

Gardner, H. (1983). *Frames of mind: The theory of multiple intelligences.* New York, NY: Basic Books.

Gleick, J. (1988). *Chaos: Making a new science.* New York, NY: Viking Press.

Goleman, D. (1998). *Working with emotional intelligence.* New York, NY: Bantam Books.

Goudge, T. A. (1967). Emergent evolutionism. In P. Edwards (Ed.), *The encyclopedia of philosophy* (Vol. 1). New York, NY: Macmillan.

Gould, S. J. (1989). *Wonderful life: The Burgess Shale and the nature of history.* New York, NY: W. W. Norton.

Gould, S. J. (2002). *The structure of evolutionary theory.* Cambridge, MA: Harvard University Press.

Greenberg, J. R., & Mitchell, S. A. (1983). *Object relations in psychoanalytic theory.* Cambridge, MA: Harvard University Press.

Guerin, P., & Pendagast, E. (1976). Evaluation of family system and genogram. In P. Guerin (Ed.), *Family therapy: Theory and practice.* New York, NY: Gardner Press.

Haley, J. (1973). *Uncommon therapy: The psychiatric techniques of Milton H. Erickson, M.D.* New York, NY: W. W. Norton.

Harari, Y. N. (2015). *Sapiens: A brief history* of humankind. New York: Harper.

Harari, Y. N. (2017). *Homo Deus: A brief history of tomorrow.* New York: HarperCollins.

Harari, Y. N. (2019). *21 lessons for the 21st century.* New York: Penguin Random House.

Hobbes, T. (2018). *Leviathan*. Hollywood, FL: Simon & Brown. (Originally published 1651).

Hoffman, L. (1981). *Foundations of family therapy: A conceptual framework for system change*. New York, NY: Basic Books.

Izard, C. (1977). *Human emotions*. New York, NY: Plenum Press.

Kaplan, R.S. & Norton, D.P. (1992, Jan.-Feb.). The Balanced Scorecard—Measures that drive performance. *Harvard Business Review*. Retrieved from https://hbr.org/1992/01/the-balanced-scorecard-measures-that-drive-performance-2

Kaplan, R.S. and Norton, D.P. (1996). Using the Balanced Scorecard as a strategic management system. *Harvard Business Review*. Retrieved from https://hbr.org/2007/07/using-the-balanced-scorecard-as-a-strategic-management-system

Kernberg, O. F. (1985). The couch at sea: Psychoanalytic studies of group and organizational leadership. In A. D. Colman & M. H. Geller (Eds.), *Group relations reader 2* (pp. 399–411). Washington, DC: A. K. Rice Institute. (Original work published 1984)

Klein, M. (1975). Notes on some schizoid mechanisms. In author (Ed.), *Envy and gratitude and other works, 1946–1963*. New York, NY: Delacorte Press. (Original work published in 1946)

Koch, S. (1976). Language communities, search cells, and the psychological studies. In W. J. Arnold (Ed.), *Nebraska Symposium on Motivation, 1975: Vol. 23*. Lincoln, NE: University of Nebraska Press.

Koestler, A., & Smythies, J. R. (Eds.). (1969). *The Alpbach Symposium 1968: Beyond Reductionism: New Perspectives in the Life Sciences.* London, United Kingdom: Hutchinson.

Koestler, A. (1978). *Janus: A summing up.* New York, NY: Random House.

Krantz, J., & Gilmore, T. N. (1991). Understanding the dynamics between consulting teams and client systems. In M. F. R. Kets de Vries, & associates (Eds.), *Organizations on the couch: Clinical perspectives on organizational behavior and change* (pp. 307–330). San Francisco, CA: Jossey-Bass.

LeBon, G. (1982). *The crowd: A study of the popular mind.* New York, NY: Cherokee. (Original work published 1896)

Leiberman, M., Yalom, I. D., & Miles, M. B. (1973). *Encounter groups: First facts.* New York, NY: Basic Books.

Levenson, E. A. (1972). *The fallacy of understanding: An inquiry into the changing structure of psychoanalysis.* New York, NY: Basic Books.

Levenson, E. A. (1991). *The purloined self: Interpersonal perspectives in psychoanalysis.* New York, NY: Contemporary Psychoanalysis Books.

Lewin, K. (1951). *Field theory in social science.* New York, NY: Harper & Row.

Lovelock, J. (1988). *Gaia: A new look at life on earth.* New York, NY: Oxford University Press.

Margulis, L., Sagan, D., & Mayr, E. (2002). *Acquiring genomes: A theory of the origins of species.* New York, NY: Basic Books.

Maturana, H. R., & Varela, F. J. (1987). *The tree of knowledge: The biological roots of human understanding.* Boston, MA: Shambhala.

Mayr, E. (1970). *Population, species, and evolution.* Cambridge, MA: Harvard University Press.

Medawar, J. S., & Medawar, P. (1983). *Aristotle to zoos: A philosophical dictionary of biology.* Cambridge, MA: Harvard University Press.

Miller, E. J., & Rice, A. K. (1967). *Systems of organization.* London, United Kingdom: Tavistock.

Millsap, A. (2018, November 27). Why General Motors is leaving Lordstown and what's next. *Forbes.* Retrieved from https://www.forbes.com/sites/adammillsap/2018/11/27/why-general-motors-is-leaving-lordstown-and-whats-next/#440221e6441c

Minuchin, S., & Fishman, H. C. (1981). *Family therapy techniques.* Cambridge, MA: Harvard University Press.

Mitchell, S. A. (1979). Twilight of the idols. *Contemporary Psychoanalysis, 15,* 170–189.

Munroe, R. L. (1955). *Schools of psychoanalytic thought: An exposition, critique, and attempt at integration.* New York, NY: Holt, Rinehart and Winston.

Nunneley, P. (2001). *The biodynamic philosophy and treatment of psychosomatic conditions.* New York, NY: Peter Lang.

Pam, A. (1993). Family systems theory—A critical view. *New Ideas in Psychology, 11,* 77–94.

Phillips, D. C. (1976). *Holistic thought in social science.* Stanford, CA: Stanford University Press.

Pink, D. (1998). *Free agent nation.* Cambridge, MA: Harvard University Press.

Pinker, S. (2011) *The better angels of our nature: Why violence has declined.* New York: Viking.

Pollan, M. (2001). *The botany of desire: A plant's-eye view of the world.* New York, NY: Random House.

Prigogine, I., & Stengers, I. (with Toffler, A.). (1984). *Order out of chaos: Man's new dialogue with nature.* New York, NY: Bantam Books.

Redlich, F. C., & Freedman, D. X. (1966). *The theory and practice of psychiatry.* New York, NY: Basic Books.

Rice, A. K. (1963). *The enterprise and its environment.* London, United Kingdom: Tavistock.

Rice, A. K. (1965). *Learning for leadership.* London, United Kingdom: Tavistock.

Rothschild, M. (1992). *Bionomics: Economy as ecosystem.* New York, NY: Henry Holt.

Senge, P. M. (1994). *The fifth discipline.* New York, NY: Currency/Doubleday.

Senge, P. M., Kleiner, A., Roberts, C., Ross, R., & Smith, B. (Eds.). (1994). *The fifth discipline fieldbook: Strategies and tools for building a learning organization.* New York, NY: Currency/Doubleday.

Shannon, C. E., & Weaver, W. (1963). *Mathematical theory of communication.* Urbana, IL: University of Illinois. (Original work published 1949)

Shapiro, E. C. (1995). *Fad surfing in the boardroom: Managing in the age of instant answers.* New York, NY: Perseus.

Simon, H. A. (1960). *The new science of management decision.* New York, NY: Harper & Brothers.

Sirkin, M. I. (1990a). Cult involvement: A systems approach to assessment and treatment. *Psychotherapy: Theory, Research, Practice, 27,* 116–123.

Sirkin, M. I. (1990b, July). *The extremist group: An analysis of its internal dynamics.* Paper presented at the meeting of the Annual Meeting of the International Society of Political Psychology, Washington, DC.

Sirkin, M. I. (1990c, August). *The manifestations of social intelligence in young adulthood.* Paper presented at the meeting of the American Psychological Association, Boston, MA.

Sirkin, M. I. (1991). Academy of space studies: Planning for a spacefaring future. In J. Mayer (Ed.), *Proceedings of the Seventh Annual International Space Development Conference: Space: The Next Renaissance.* San Diego, CA: Univelt.

Sirkin, M. I. (1992a). *On consulting to selves, groups, and corporate communities: From interpersonal theory to dynamic systems theory.* Unpublished manuscript, William Alanson White Institute, New York, NY.

Sirkin, M. I. (1992b). *Structure and process in living systems: An introduction to dynamic systems theory.* Unpublished manuscript, Ferkauf Graduate School of Psychology, Yeshiva University, New York, NY.

Sirkin, M. I. (1994a). Clinical issues in intermarriage: A family systems approach, Part I: An overview of theoretical and ethical issues. *Journal of Jewish Communal Service, 70,* 271–282.

Sirkin, M. I. (1994b). Clinical issues in intermarriage: A family systems approach, Part II: Technical issues in the clinical treatment of intermarriage. *Journal of Jewish Communal Service, 71,* 74–86.

Sirkin, M. I. (1994c, August). *Dynamic systems theory: Toward integrating theory and practice.* Paper presented at the meeting of the 102nd Annual Convention of the American Psychological Association, Los Angeles, CA.

Sirkin, M. I. (1996). Consulting to family business: The dollars and sense of family values. *The Family Therapy Networker, 20,* 71–78.

Sirkin, M. I., & Fleming, M. (1982). Freud's "Project" and its relationship to psychoanalytic theory. *Journal of the History of the Behavioral Sciences, 18,* 230–241.

Sirkin, M. I., & Sirkin, M. W. (1994, August). *Mapping values in family businesses: A technique for consultants.* Paper presented at the meeting of the 102nd Annual Convention of the American Psychological Association, Los Angeles, CA.

Sirkin, M. I., & Wynne, L. C. (1990). Cult involvement as relational disorder. *Psychiatric Annals, 20,* 199–203.

Smith, A. (2016). *The wealth of nations.* Hollywood, FL: Simon & Brown. (Originally published 1776).

Smith, A.G. (2016, July 6). Price gouging and the dangerous new breed of pharma companies. *Harvard Business Review.* Retrieved from https://hbr.org/2016/07/price-gouging-and-the-dangerous-new-breed-of-pharma-companies

Stout, L. (2012). *The shareholder value myth: How putting shareholders first harms investors, corporations, and the public.* Oakland, CA: Berrett-Koehler Publishers.

Strine, L. E. (2014) Making it easier for directors to do the right thing, *Harvard Business Law Review* (pp. 235 – 253).

Sullivan, H. S. (1953). *The interpersonal theory of psychiatry.* New York, NY: W. W. Norton.

Teilhard de Chardin, P. (1965) *The phenomenon of man.* New York, NY: Harper.

Tapscott, D. (1996). *The digital economy: Promise and peril in the age of networked intelligence.* New York, NY: McGraw-Hill.

Thun, M. (2000). *Gardening for life—The biodynamic way.* Stroud, United Kingdom: Hawthorn Press.

Trist, E. L., & Murray, H. (Eds.). (1990). *The social engagement of social science: The Tavistock anthology.* Philadelphia, PA: University of Pennsylvania Press von Bertalanffy, L. (1968). *General systems theory: Foundations, developments, applications.* New York, NY: Brazilier.

Wagner, R. R. (2000). Virus. In *Encyclopaedia Britannica* (2000 deluxe ed.). [CD]. Chicago, IL: Encyclopaedia Britannica. (Original work published 1994–2000)

Waldrop, M. M. (1992). *Complexity: The emerging science at the edge of order and chaos.* New York, NY: Simon & Schuster.

Wheatley, M. J. (2001). *Leadership and the new science: Discovering order in a chaotic world* (2nd ed.) San Francisco, CA: Berrett-Koehler. (Original work published 1992)

Wiener, N. (1963). *Cybernetics, second edition: or the control and communication in the animal and the machine.* Cambridge, MA: MIT Press. (Original work published 1959)

Wilson, E. O. (1971). *The insect societies.* Cambridge, MA: The Belknap Press of Harvard University Press.

Wilson, E. O. (1998). *Consilience: The unity of knowledge.* New York, NY: Knopf.

Wilson, E. O. (1999). *The diversity of life.* New York, NY: W. W. Norton.

Winkler, A. (2019). *We the corporations: How American businesses won their civil rights.* New York: Liveright Publishing Corporation.

Wynne, L. C., McDaniel, S. H., & Weber, T. T. (Eds.). (1986). *Systems consultation: A new perspective for family therapy.* New York, NY: The Guilford Press.

Printed in the United States
By Bookmasters